D0089131

About this book

In this book, Zillah Eisenstein continues her unforgiving indictment of neoliberal imperial politics. She charts its most recent militarist and masculinist configurations through discussions of the Afghan and Iraq wars, violations at Guantanamo and Abu Ghraib, the 2004 US Presidential election, and Hurricane Katrina. She warns that women's rights rhetoric is being manipulated, particularly by Condoleezza Rice and other women in the Bush administration, as a ploy for global dominance and a misogynistic capture of democratic discourse. However, Eisenstein also believes that the plural and diverse lives of women will lay the basis for an assault on these fascistic elements. This new politics will both confound and clarify feminisms, and reconfigure democracy across the globe.

About the author

Zillah Eisenstein is one of the foremost political theorists and activists of our time. She has written feminist theory in North America for the past twenty-five years. Her writing is an integral part of her political activism. She writes in order to share and learn with, and from, others engaged in political struggles for social justice. She writes about her work building coalitions across women's differences: the black/white divide in the US; the struggles of Serb and Muslim women in the war in Bosnia; the needs of women health workers in Cuba; the commitments of environmentalists in Ghana; the relationship between socialists and feminists in union organizing; the struggles against extremist fundamentalisms in Egypt and Afghanistan; the needs of women workers in India.

Zillah Eisenstein is Professor of Politics at Ithaca College in New York. Throughout her career her books have tracked the rise of neoliberalism both within the US and across the globe. She has documented the demise of liberal democracy and scrutinized the growth of imperial and militarist globalization. She has also critically written about the attack on affirmative action in the US, the masculinist bias of law, the crisis of breast cancer and AIDS, the racism of patriarchy and the patriarchal structuring of race, the new nationalisms, and corporatist multiculturalism.

Her most recent books include: *Against Empire* (London, Zed Books, 2004), *Hatreds: Racialised and Sexualised Conflicts in the 21st Century* (New York, Routledge, 1996), *Global Obscenities: Patriarchy, Capitalism and the Lure of Cyberfantasy* (New York, NYU Press, 1998), *ManMade Breast Cancers* (Ithaca, Cornell University Press, 2001).

Sexual Decoys

*Gender, Race and War
in Imperial Democracy*

Zillah Eisenstein

Spinifex Press
MELBOURNE

Zed Books
LONDON & NEW YORK

Sexual Decoys: Gender, Race and War in Imperial Democracy was first published in 2007 by
Zed Books Ltd, 7 Cynthia Street, London N1 9JF, UK and
Room 400, 175 Fifth Avenue, New York, NY 10010, USA
www.zedbooks.co.uk

Published in Australia and New Zealand by Spinifex Press, 504 Queensberry Street
PO Box 212, North Melbourne, Victoria 3051, Australia
www.spinifexpress.com.au

Cover designed by Andrew Corbett
Set in 11/13 pt Perpetua by Long House, Cumbria, UK
Printed and bound in Malta by Gutenberg Press Ltd

Distributed in the USA exclusively by Palgrave Macmillan, a division of
St Martin's Press, LLC,175 Fifth Avenue, New York, NY 10010

ISBN 10:   1 84277 816 1 hb
ISBN 10:   1 84277 817 X pb
ISBN 13:   978 1 84277 816 6 hb
ISBN 13:   978 1 84277 817 3 pb
ISBN 10: 1-876756-63-2 pb (Spinifex)
ISBN 13: 978-1-876756-63-5 pb (Spinifex)

Contents

Acknowledgments

So many people have been a part of the writing of this book. Some have spoken with me about its ideas; others have read portions of the manuscript at different stages and shared their responses; others have written work that has impacted on my thinking; others have accompanied me on my travels; others have organized and attended political marches and demonstrations that I write about here; others have dialogued from afar by email; others have pointed me to new work; others have extended deep friendship. Some have done all these things. This book could not have been written without these individuals and the communities they inhabit. A deep thank-you to: Miriam Brody, Susan Buck-Morss, Rosalind Petchesky, Ellen Wade, Chandra Talpade Mohanty, Rebecca Riley, Carla Golden, Naeem Inayatalluh, Asma Barlas, Judith Butler, Joan Romm, Anne Fausto-Sterling, Bernadette Muthien, Patty Zimmermann, Kavita Panjabi, Sandra Greene, Angana Chatterji, Shareen Gokal, Meyda Yegenoglu, Cynthia Enloe, Anna Marie Smith, Valentine Moghadam, Mary Katzenstein, Ella Shohat, Donald Dawsland, Paisley Currah, Tilu Bal, Tom Shevory, and Mary Ryan.

I want to note some extraordinary devotion. Miriam has read all my work for these many years, and once again has read the entirety of the manuscript, and some parts several times. Susan has engaged with this project from the start with enormous enthusiasm, and has read and commented on the full draft. Carla has read particular sections, sometimes with no turn-around time, so that they could quickly be used for internet distribution. She also was crucial to my work in collecting signatures against the HR 3077 initiative to curtail academic area studies programs, and she marched with me against the war. Naeem offered me a continual and provocative ear whenever I needed it as I grappled with deciphering my complicated thoughts about decoys; and also marched with me against the war, with his son Kamal. Asma shared her brilliant engagement with all things Islamic to make sure I was not being ignorant of nuance. Ros continued to share her fabulous ways of thinking with me as I wrote my way through these years of war turmoil. Chandra shares her thoughts and herself even when Uma gives her no time to do so.

None of my thinking or my writing or my believing that are a part of this book would be possible without the women's activism and feminist movements that struggle and thrive in Thailand, Cuba, Korea, Turkey, Palestine, India, South Africa, Ghana, Spain, Chile, Afghanistan, and Iraq.

I am not sure that I would be able to think the way I do about sexual borders and traversing them if not for my friendship with Donald Dawsland. He defies category while celebrating his sexual being with courage, always.

My deepest thanks to Tsveta Petrova, my Cornell research assistant, who was always generous with her time and energy and was amazing. I very often was looking for documents that could not be found, and she always found them. Thanks as well to Provost Peter Bardaglio of Ithaca College for his research funding and exceptional support for my work and travel.

I want to recognize the important distribution of my writings about Abu Ghraib, the Supreme Court nominees, hurricane Katrina, and the 2005 anti-Iraq-war march at: *www.WHRnet.org* and *www.nwsa.org/katrina*.

And of course this book would have not happened without the support of my editor Anna Hardman, and Julian Hosie and Farouk Sohawan at Zed Books. Special thanks to my copyeditor, Pat Harper.

Thanks to my Gender and Militarism seminars at Ithaca College, 2004–6, and to McMaster University, Hamilton, Ontario; Harvard University Law School, Cambridge, Massachusetts; METU University, Ankara, Turkey; Trinity College, Dublin, Ireland, for inviting me to share this work as it was in process.

Deep thanks to Bernie Wohl, Carmen Lewis and Sheila Davidson for their love and attention to my miraculous mother in these last years.

Deepest thanks to Richard Stumbar for his extraordinary love and friendship and his companionship on most of my travels; and to Sarah Eisenstein Stumbar for being my fabulous daughter who brings endless joy to me in all things. My sister Julia Price Eisenstein nurtures my soul in miraculous ways despite her daily life of physical pain.

... to all those who risk hoping for new ways of being

Preface

January 2006 is a hard month. Snow covers the ground but it is iced and dirty, not new and clean. It is cold … and with gas and fuel at record highs in the US, most of us are living chillier lives than before. The recent past has included the exposing of the torture at Abu Ghraib, the re-election of George Bush, and then the horrors of the tsunami and hurricane Katrina with their continuing devastation. The American public is told that our president has secretly authorized the National Security Agency to eavesdrop on us as the wars in Afghanistan and Iraq limp forward. There is greater surveillance, while dissent is criminalized. More and more is made visible and visual, while there is less and less power to change the picture.

I start here with a heavy heart to uncover the new in these 'new-old' scenarios.[1] I look to trace and uncover the racialized and gendered silenced stories of this militarized moment of global capitalist racialized patriarchy. These entire scenarios are man-made by so-called manly men – but men can be either male or female, white or 'other-than'. Racialized gender operates as a decoy. Men can be male-identified males *or* females given that there are male- and female-bodied men. As such, there are more than two sexes and more than two genders and yet politically we are said and made to be male and female, man and woman.

So sex and gender and race can be used as decoys because their meanings can always be multiple and varied at the same time that they are ossified. Sex and gender, though distinct and multiple, are more often than not collapsed as one. The variations of femaleness and femininity, and maleness and masculinity, stand counter to the homogeneity of heteronormative gender. This creates confusing, illegible, and unknowable readings and meanings.[2] The unreadable aspects of sex, gender, and race allow for their deceptive role today as sometime decoys for imperial and fascistic democracy. But gender cannot always or completely be deceiving or it would not work as a decoy. This increases the difficulty of reading the meanings of sex and gender and race. The complex decoy process – of allure, deception, and entrapment – defines history and also takes on 'new–old' historical meanings. War makes these processes more visible and contested. It is this racializing and gendering of politics that I wish to see more clearly for today. Yet the language itself almost makes it impossible to think with these complexities.

I am looking for 'unthinkable facts', needing new 'instruments of thought', wanting to conceptualize without the categories to do so.[3] There is female and male masculinity; and male and female femininity. Condoleezza Rice embodies this decoy status as she makes war for white men. And veiled Muslim women become the decoys of and for wars of terror – by both imperial and Islamic insurgent misogynists. Read on if this is not clear to you.

My focus now is to see how the particular moment of war and militarism continues to transform and reconfigure the meaning of gender along with its relationship to the sexed and raced body. I look to explain and reveal the newest fluidities of gender that disconnect the meanings of the female body from its gendered formation. So more females today are in the military, are affected by wars, are militarized in their private lives, are in fighting forces in third-world countries, are immigrants and refugees, and this destabilizes entrenched gender meanings while the privilege of a racialized masculinism also remains in place, even if changed. While using women's rights discourse as a cover and ploy for global dominance, females like Condi Rice and Hillary Clinton articulate the newest imperial democracy that only further complicates things.

This *may* be a critical historical juncture where gender will be truly destabilized with the help of feminisms across the globe; *or* masculinist formulations of gender in defense of imperial democracy may hold sway but in more variegated forms. In just the past year there have been a series of firsts: women have been elected president in Chile, Germany, and Liberia, Cecelia Fire Thunder has been elected leader of the Oglala Sioux tribe, Tzipi Livni serves as the first Israeli foreign minister since Golda Meir, and six women were elected to the newly chosen Hamas parliament. The meanings of each of these happenings are not clearly obvious. Some of these victories reflect enormous political struggle and achievement. Each of my chapters deals with different aspects of the making of sexes and genders and races; the gendering of war, the militarizing of gender, and the multiplicity of patriarchies and therefore feminisms. Gender remains incredibly complex and confused amidst these changes. On the one hand so much is changing ... and on the other it is not clear what exactly is changed.

Greater varieties and expressions of gender and sexuality exist for my daughter than did for me; women are present in new and different sites; patriarchy is more differentiated and complex, creating more choice and variability; and there are also greater restrictions on many of the choices given neoliberal privatization across the globe. It is harder to get an abortion today in the US than a decade ago. More male and female teenagers engage in oral sex today and say that this is not sex. In the fall of 2005 a TV series – *Commander-in-Chief* – was broadcast about a woman president. Yet, females have not regendered the military. And the wars of/on terror often morph into talk about sex and gender while conflating them.

I trace the development of gender fluidity and racial diversity, rather than equality, in this militarized moment as oftentimes anti-democratic. And I will argue that the diversity that exists within women's lives today across the globe should not be confused with sexual or gender equality or justice and that it also sometimes means exactly this. And that the co-optation of racial diversity of the few, for the displacement of racial equality for the many, underpins the horrific moves towards right-wing fanaticism. So there are the processes of resexing gender – females acting like men; re-gendering gender – women becoming more modern and diverse as women; e-racing race – blacks becoming Clarence Thomas or Colin Powell; re-racing race – black women becoming white. Do not mis-interpret these political processes as essentialist and static. The brilliance is in the constant exceptionalism. The difficulty is with essentializing cat-egories that I mean to displace.

President Bush did not mention the Iraq war in his 2005 inaugural address and instead focused all eyes on his struggle for freedom and liberty – at home and abroad. "The survival of liberty in our land increas-ingly depends on the success of liberty in other lands." He said that America will not impose our own style of government on the unwilling, because they must find their own way and voice.[4] He promised to bring unity to the country – despite the so-called blue (liberal) and red (con-servative) states. His democratic message codes politics as war. Within a few months, as discontent for the war mounts, speaking at the National

Endowment for Democracy he is more defensive and aggressive although not more truthful. "We will not rest until the war on terror is won." He says the choices are simple: between freedom's triumph or Islamic radicalism and its militant Jihadism/Islamo-fascism. He reiterates his stance again – that the US will never back down and will accept nothing less than complete victory. He speaks of the "murderous" ideology of Islamic radicals and compares it to the struggle against communism, also an ideology with "cold-blooded contempt for human life". Islamic radicals have ambitions of "imperial domination" while they "brutalize their women". Iraq is the launching pad for all that is evil. America will stay the course.[5] By March 2006, with support for the war waning, Bush is very much more on the defensive.

On October 8, 2005 the US public awaited the indictments of Scooter Libby and Karl Rove for their role in leaking information about a CIA agent – Valerie Palme – the wife of Joseph Wilson, in order to punish him for challenging Bush's claims about Saddam's weapons of mass destruction. This same morning National Public Radio (NPR) led with a news story charging the CIA with the murder and torture of detainees held in the Afghan and Iraq wars. On the one hand the US government appears rational and legal as it charges offenders with lying; and on the other hand torture and death are condoned. This is what neoliberal fascism, or fascistic democracy, must look like; what militant global capitalism necessitates. The war on terror has destroyed the remnants of democracy through the militarization of us all. The always troubled emancipatory rhetoric dating back to the Enlightenment appears to have been *almost entirely* displaced by terror rhetoric.

Once again I am at a loss for words to help me think. There is little new in the claim that liberal/Western/bourgeois democracy has never been fully democratic, or that it is wrong to conflate Western-style democracy with democracy itself.[6] Today, neoliberal forms of democracy parade as though they too are one and the same with democracy and position themselves against Islam as such. Although Western democracy has an imperial past and present, it also now newly articulates fascistic neoliberal practices. I use both 'neoliberal fascism' and 'fascistic democracy' as terms of alarm for present tendencies in the US. Although these tendencies may appear to be exceptions, they also can too easily become the rule. The slide from and between neoliberal and fascistic democracy can only be seen from particular sites.

Many Germans said they did not know about the extermination of more than 6 million Jews during Nazism. For them, ordinary life continued. Today ordinary life continues for many of us in the US while it does not continue as such for those detained elsewhere, or those who are wire-tapped, or incarcerated in Guantanamo. Whether one calls these actions exceptions – to the rule of law – depends upon where one is located and from what position one speaks. This kind of exceptionalism leads towards the newly forming fascistic democracy, and away from an Enlightenment liberal and neoliberal reading constrained by the promise of legal rights for all.

The wars in Afghanistan and Iraq are destroying the soul of America. Bombs are dropped indiscriminately, bodies are maimed, prisoners of war have no rights, Guantanamo continues to house inmates illegally. Tsunamis and hurricanes ravage poor people's lives and the US government offers belated charity but not social justice. Katrina uncovers racism and poverty that many in the US say they did not know existed, and I wonder if Halliburton will once again be the true beneficiary of all this misery.

The new lawlessness of the Bush administration both at home and abroad fully neglects democratic discourse. The newness locates today's enemies at home as much as abroad. Muslims, South Asians, Latinas, El Salvadoreans, Pakistanis, Somalians are located in New York, New Jersey, Minnesota, California. Those who came to America to escape violence and persecution now wonder where that America has gone. Since September 11, 2001 they have lost the freedom they came here seeking. They say that our prisons and detention centers are worse than the refugee camps they have been in elsewhere. War rhetoric has licensed new undemocratic processes: from racial profiling to enforced registrations, to racist round-ups and deportations.[7]

To the rest of the world, the US, especially since the Abu Ghraib scandal, no longer stands for human rights doctrine, no matter how limited the actual practice may have been earlier. We are no longer as welcoming a nation to the world's migrants, exiles, and refugees. In the name of 'security' we mistake people in need for criminals and terrorists. As Edwidge Danticat says of her ageing Haitian uncle: "My uncle was treated like a criminal when his only offense was thinking that he could find shelter in the United States." She continues: "A zone is being locked in place on the outer perimeter of the United States where the constitution is no longer fully operable."[8]

We are becoming more unlike our better selves as exceptions are made. To the wife and son of a man the CIA detained, tortured, and killed in Afghanistan, the US government is no different than fascists. Racialized gender and sex operate as both cover and deception – as though democracy exists because Colin Powell and Condoleezza Rice exist – and as exposure – as in the sexual and racial violations in the prisons of Guantanamo and Abu Ghraib. Amidst this cacophony it is no longer clear, if it ever was, who or what a woman is, and/or what it means or should mean to be African American. Color trumps race; gender trumps sex. And, patriarchal/racialized hetero-masculinity has authorized and normalized a privileged white womanhood.

Females like Condi Rice and Sandra Day O'Connor do the bidding of imperial power while women and girls join militaries almost everywhere as part of the newly militarized global economy. The new diversity of choice for gender sites, alongside their racialized identities, defines this militarized historical moment. The economy runs strong for only a very few. Everyone I know seems to be driven and too busy. Professional jobs are being restructured and changed and we pretend that they are the same. Work of all sorts is leaving the country for elsewheres. The wars in Afghanistan and Iraq make no sense no matter what your politics is and yet they continue. We are exposed as humiliators and torturers and continue with arrogance to do the same.

There is less accountability as the nation-state is privatized for the needs of global capital. The newly defined wars of/on terror have undermined the nation which was a key site for articulating racialized gender. This undermining, or reconfiguring, of the nation loosens and deregulates the patriarchal site of 'the' family. Hence the transitional and conflictual relationship within and between the relations of public and private life.

With militarization everywhere, given the wars of/on terror previous notions of war, peace, civilian, and combatant are dislocated along with the rigidity of gender and race. A militarized economy rooted in war constructs new rules for neoliberal and fascistic imperial democracy. Global capital, with its need for privatization, becomes less and less able to afford the messiness of democracy. Just-in-time flexible and fluid configurations are always constructed from the vantage point of the powerful.

War is fictionalized as spectacular and exceptional rather than common and everyday and personal. Many of us privileged at the site of empire can remain removed and distant. In the US, too many can keep from wondering how people survive in Iraq, or how they themselves would survive if they were there. So Cindy Sheehan, the now well-known mother of a son, Casey, who was killed in Iraq, camped outside Bush's Crawford, Texas, ranch demanding to speak with him. She publicized the war as up-close and personal. She was arrested at the 2006 State of the Union address because she was wearing a T-shirt reading: 2244 DEAD. She says later of the arrest that she wept because she has lost not only her son Casey, but also her First Amendment rights and with them the country she has loved.[9]

Riverbend, the young Iraqi woman writing a daily blog, describes the dreariness of everyday life in war. She writes about the lack of electricity and water, about the unrelenting heat, and the night-time raids which meant people went to bed in their clothes, and the shortages of gasoline and its high cost. She writes of the daily life that doesn't happen, the daily routines that no longer exist. War is not just about dying; it is about living a life that isn't worth living. She says of Iraq that "no one is 13 anymore"; that everyone is 85.[10]

In the US there is more and more control of everything – even our memory, or lack of it. The militarization of everyday life has people fearful rather than emboldened. We watch the devastation produced by hurricane Katrina and floods in Mississippi and Alabama and find it 'unspeakable'. The racism, the poverty, the huge numbers of displaced women and children of the poor are unthinkable. As Jenny Edkins writes, we lack a language to help us with our betrayal by our country. "After traumatic events, there is a struggle over memory. Some forms of remembering can be seen as ways of forgetting..."[11] Bush used the Katrina tragedy to call for greater militarization, suggesting that it would be preferable for the military to be in charge when natural/national disasters hit. Militia rule for New Orleans.

The amount of mediation between our bodies and the rule of law, as in torture, is disregarded. Lying has replaced misrepresentation. The notion of 'normal juridical order' is less and less clear; and the 'state of exception' has started to become the rule.[12] The US government has moved beyond the rule of law while policing the world with impunity. There is total control of media, and the control is not exactly total.

The conceptual deficit that disallows the naming of racialized gender as central to the reconfigurations of power allows its decoy status for anti-democratic rule. More women and people of color are to be seen everywhere. This is the truth and falsity of the globe. The manipulation of race and gender as decoys for democracy reveals the corruptibility of identity politics. Not until women had the vote could they know its insufficiencies for changing their lives. Not until civil rights movement activists gained an end to legal discrimination could they know its insufficiencies for ending racism. Not until apartheid was ended in South Africa could blacks know its full complexities. And not until militarism is seen for its masculinist heteronormative gendering can war be viewed as always anti-thetical to peace; or the full complex array of feminisms which imagine a socially just, inclusive world come into view.

Notes

1   See my *Global Obscenities: Patriarchy, Capitalism, and the Lure of Cyberfantasy* (New York: New York University Press, 1998) for a discussion of how the new is always historically connected to the old in the phrasing 'new-old'.

2   For a compelling discussion of the historical unreadability of multiple sexualities see: Afsaneh Najmabadi, *Women with Mustaches and Men without Beards* (Berkeley: University of California Press, 2005).

3   Michel-Rolph Trouillot, *Silencing the Past* (Boston: Beacon, 1995), p. 82.

4   *www.whitehouse.gov/inaugural/January* 20, 2005.

5   *www.whitehouse.gov/news/releases/2005/10/20051006-3.html*.

6   C.B. MacPherson, *Democratic Theory: Essays in Retrieval* (Oxford: Clarendon Press, 1973).

7   Tram Nguyen, ed., *We Are All Suspects Now: Untold Stories from Immigrant Communities after 9/11* (Boston: Beacon Press, 2005), pp. 80–81.

8   Edwidge Danticat, "Not Your Homeland", *The Nation*, vol. 281, no. 9 (September 26, 2005), pp. 23, 26. See also her foreword in Tram Nguyen, ed., *We Are All Suspects Now*.

9   Cindy Sheehan, "What Really Happened", February 2, 2006, at *www.truthout.org/docs*.

10   Riverbend, *Baghdad Burning* (New York: Feminist Press, 2005), p. 11. See also: *http://riverbendblog.blogspot.com/*.

11   Jenny Edkins, *Trauma and the Memory of Politics* (London: Cambridge University Press, 2003), p. 16.

12   Giorgio Agamben. "Means Without End: Notes on Politics", *Theory Out Of Bounds*, vol. 20 (University of Minnesota Press, 1994), p. 38.

1
Gender as Politics in Another Form

In December 2003 the US was on code orange alert. Air France canceled its Christmas Eve flights because of information that they might be used to 'hit' targets in New York City or Los Angeles. Meanwhile *The Last Samurai* played in theatres romanticizing the Eastern warrior – through the visor of yoga and life's harmony – and humanized war in Eastern fashion. Death – in war – is honorable despite the fact that the samurai fights on behalf of the emperor and other hierarchies of power. The wife of the slain samurai falls in love with his killer. She is deferential and suffering and therefore noble as well. *Elephant* also played in our theatres. It tells the story of the massacre at Columbine High School and the sad effects of a militarized culture. This same season the Vietnam War is the backdrop for explaining the unexplainable in life in *The Human Stain*, a story about racial self-hatred and passing for white while black.

In 2004 a remake of *The Manchurian Candidate* is produced. It is a story about a fictional right-wing senator who happens to be both female and a mother. She manipulates and betrays her son, and abandons all morals to create a world of complete surveillance and mind control. In the remade film we see people having their brains drilled for implants and total manipulation, and I cannot help but wonder if this is a form of the mindlessness that allowed Bush his second term. And I wonder if the film is a kind of whitewash: that filmgoers look at this depiction of the world and fantasize that they are free because they are not having their brains drilled.

In 2005, *King Kong* is remade in old form. The beast and natives are still black but made more horrific and terrifying by new digital tech. The beauty is still white and blonde. Misogyny is still the trope: warring factions define human life, be they digital dinosaurs or unfathomable creatures or helpless white men. Females still love anything that protects them.

In real life, war rages in Afghanistan and Iraq but as a backdrop and not front and center. These wars are mired in discourses about democracy and women's rights to be free from abusive lives under the Taliban or Saddam Hussein. Neither of these wars were committed to freeing women so it remains critically important to think through why these were the particular narratives at this specific point in historic time.

Human rights – and with them women's rights – have been used to mystify and rationalize the misogynist and racialized aspects of global capitalism. Women's rights as a discourse both legitimizes democracy and critiques other-than-Western forms of democracy simultaneously. As such, women's rights parades as Western to the rest of the world. But it is closer to the truth, if there are truths to be found here, that masculinist militarism uses women's rights for right-wing agendas inside and outside the West. Right-wing fundamentalisms of all sorts – east and west – emphasize militarist agendas alongside the gendering of women's lives, with or without the veil/chador/abayya/burqa, as decoy.

Bush's wars of/on terror have authorized a culture of racial intimidation and surveillance while establishing gender confusions to mask this process. New forms of this militarized process create larger numbers of women as the refugees and displaced people of the world, as the rape victims in many locations like Sudan and Nepal, as the new warriors for the US military and as suicide bombers in Palestine and Iraq. Sometimes it looks like women are becoming more like men; if being militarized is the same as being masculinized. But I think similarity is not what is simply happening here but rather that the constructions of gender are being more fully diversified *and* essentialized simultaneously.

In this militarized setting masculinity and femininity are becoming more complex but not necessarily more equal. The redefinition looks newly different, but is more 'new-old' than new. Gender is being mobilized for new purposes and refashioned in more 'modern' fashion. Differentiation of women from men remains and yet they each occupy more like spheres in similarly different fashion. Militarized masculinity still needs a hetero-feminine gendered complement; and each keeps the other in place.[1] So gender codes the Afghan and Iraq wars. It is also not inherently biological. Gender regulates sex and sexuality that are more ambiguous than they are certain. And gender is reshaped continually in order also to shape and control sexual meanings. King Kong still lives.

On gendering sex

Gendering is the process of transforming females to women and males to men when neither of these starting points is completely autonomous from their transformed state. Gendering is a process of differentiating supposed heterosexuality – of making gendered difference matter by institutionalizing it.

It is often thought that sexuality – as in biological sex and sexual preference — is more stable, or static, and predefined, than gender. But I continue to query whether gender – as in the cultural construction of masculine and feminine – is not more static and contrived and more resistant to change.[2] In this way gender rigidifies sex; gender regulates sex and sexual preference, as much as, if not more than, the other way around. This is not to overdraw the distinctness of sex and gender but rather to query whether the body's sexuality is not more ambiguous and multiple and diverse than the constructs of gender allow. Or, put slightly differently, it is to propose that gender exists to control sex and its variability. Gender makes biological sex and sexuality static and rigid. The point: neither sex nor gender is simply essentialist or constructed; they are a complex relational mix. But, given this, the sexual body is probably more fluid than its gendered meaning. Yet the biological body – meaning both the so-called 'natural body' and its given heterosexual proclivities – are normalized as a justification for the cultural meanings of men and women. In sum: gender colonizes sex.

According to Anne Fausto-Sterling, "labeling someone a man or a woman is a social decision"; actual physical bodies blur clear boundaries. She argues that the state and legal system may have an interest in maintaining that there are only two sexes, but that "our collective biological bodies do not". She believes that "masculinity and femininity are cultural conceits"; that the "two party system" of sex is a social construction, and that male and female "stand on extreme ends of a biological continuum" with many other kinds of bodies which are a "complex mix of anatomical components". As such, our sexual bodies are "indeterminate" and therefore "policed" to become male and female.

It follows both that biology as well as gender is political and that the more gender is challenged the more rigidly sex is constructed as either male or female. This extends to hormones themselves that Fausto-Sterling says are identified as though they were sexually determinant, but rather are

These racialized silences and gender confusions are both common and unique to the militarized Abu Ghraib narrative. Abu Ghraib is a horrific exposure of what war is and does always; and of what the wars of/on terror at this particular juncture of unilateral militarized globalization look like. The sadism and humiliation are not aberrations. These vicious practices had been established early after September 11, 2001 in the Brooklyn Detention Center. Pakistani Javaid Iqbal and Egyptian Ehab Elmaghraby filed civil complaints describing their beatings there. They charge that they were sodomized with a flashlight. Violations of the human rights of prisoners in Afghanistan and Guantanamo were reported by the Red Cross to Colin Powell, Condoleezza Rice and Paul Wolfowitz, to little avail.[62] Allegations of rape at Abu Ghraib were corroborated by General Antonio Taguba.

Females are at these specific locations of power while a militarist masculinism is at its height. I am thinking that it is because these locations are unaccountable and maybe even anachronistic sites of power that women occupy them. The privatization of the military has created a lack of accountability as well as unregulated arenas where sexual rape and torture are both free – in the sense of free to do what is not expressly forbidden – and silently sanctioned by higher-ups. Secretary of Defense Rumsfeld has downsized and restructured the military and maybe females have been allowed in just as these locations of institutionalized power are being denuded. It may be why it is so easy to locate the blame at these very sites.

These women should be held responsible and accountable; but they also are being used as gender decoys. They play a role of deception and lure us into a fantasy of gender equity rather than depravity. As decoys they let us pretend that this is what democracy looks like. As decoys they create confusion by participating in the very sexual humiliation that their gender is usually victim to. This supposed gender swapping and switching leaves masculinist/racialized gender in place. Just the sex has changed; the uniform remains the same. Male or female can be a masculinized commander or imperial collaborator, while white women look like masculinist empire builders and brown men look like women and homos.

Females as gender decoys allow the fantasy that women are more equal, are found anywhere with no impediments to their choices and their lives. And the decoy works because some things have changed, and these changes are not insignificant, and these changes matter. But it does not mean that they matter in the way in which they are imaged, and orchestrated. The brilliance of females being used as decoys for democracy is that the unstable relationship between sex and gender can be deployed in their confused and fluid meanings.

There is an historical precedent here. Catherine the Great, like most of the 'emperors' of Russia in the eighteenth century, was a female who ruled as a man. A clear distinction was made between the empress's female body, and her role as 'emperor', with both military and sovereign connotations. In eighteenth-century Russia in order to "attain the throne and maintain power, the female monarchs had to display masculine behavior". The common scenario for eighteenth century palace revolution "involved a ritual transversion: a female pretender dressed up as a man". Russian female rule developed "gender transversion in order to secure and strengthen her successful, but illegitimate accession". Legitimacy required "masculine attributes". Catherine the Great used "classical masculine models of imperial power ... in order to sanction her rule".[63] This is a precedent for Margaret Thatcher and Madeleine Albright.

Whenever power and domination are exposed in their ugly form as in Abu Ghraib, the embedded sexual and racialized meanings of power are revealed. Racism and sexism are always in play together because they each construct the other. When one is revealed the other is lying in wait. Salient examples of the hybrid relation between race, sex, and gender are the O.J. Simpson trial, the Clarence Thomas confirmation hearings, the beatings of Rodney King and Abner Louima and their aftermaths. One was never sure if the issues were racialized sex or sexualized racism or whether they are ever truly separable. In the case of Abu Ghraib, racial codings are used to deeply seed gender meanings and sexual confusion to build empire.

A man who is treated like a woman becomes less than human – not a white man – like the black slave woman, and not a white woman; like the lynched black man. Muslim men, along with Jews and Semitic men of all religions, are then viewed as not virile like white men. This is somewhat like the black slave man who was forced to watch the rape of his lover or child by the master, or lynching; except that the black man is made 'different' than the white man, in his hyper- rather than homosexuality. So the black man is also lynched and mutilated/castrated. Masculinist depravity, as a political discourse and practice, can be adopted by males and/or females.

Gender decoys are females in drag and the drag allows us to think that they represent the best of democracy when they don't. Yet one could also say that all gender is a form of drag – that macho men are trying to pass as just that. In other words, some drag passes as though it is natural, as in authorized versions of masculinity and femininity. Gender is already in place when females are defined as feminine; the gendering of the body controls the interpretative lens.

Laura Bush has morphed into a 'desperate housewife' by her own admission. She delivers jokes about her husband at a May 2005 black tie affair complaining that he goes to bed by eight o'clock, with the obvious implication that he leaves her sexually in need. She goes to Africa to do the US's bidding in Africa – to show the world "how good America is". She no longer is marketed to us as the dutiful wife; but rather as the activist humanist and defender of women's rights abroad. Neither Laura nor authorized gender versions remain constant. Flux and flexibility are the rule here – for patriarchal relations and for global capital.

Laura's husband, the president of the US, stays home to oversee the unsuccessful wars of/on terror. While overseeing the domestic realm he nominates two women, one black and one white, to the federal bench. Each decries affirmative action; one of them, Janice Rogers Brown, the African American daughter of a sharecropper, sees a "form of slavery in liberalism" – where government regulation fosters dependency like slavery did.[64] A female in black skin speaks out against the very tradition that gave her rights to be free and a federal judge. She is a racialized gender decoy.

Simultaneously, Republicans in Congress were forced to backtrack on requiring the Pentagon to ask Congress to vote each time the military wanted to open new battlefield support jobs to women. The military argued that the policy was too restrictive because flexibility was needed in assigning women to support units during war.[65] While women's gender roles are debated in the US, Bush speaks on behalf of women's rights in Jordan and Israel. And the gender hypocrisy continues as Republicans try to block amendments to the military authorization bill that would remove ideological barriers to providing good health care to military women who are victims of sexual assault. Finally, a narrow exception was made to allow the morning-after pill or abortion in these cases. The resistance to change crafts the debate about women in combat: women as of 1994 were prohibited from serving in direct combat units but women are allowed to fly attack helicopters and attack aircraft that provide close air support.[66] So more women are dying – four women were killed in Falluja in June 2005 when a suicide bomber struck their convoy – while the mythic divide between combat and support roles remains rigidly in place.

It is all the more despicable that the Bush administration used the language of women's rights to justify the bombs in the Afghan war by Taliban practices towards women; and then again to justify the bombing in Iraq by the horrific torture and rape chambers under Saddam Hussein.[67] And it should be no surprise that Bush's cowgirls – Laura, Mary Matalin, and Karen Hughes – who regularly dismiss and criticize feminism of any sort were responsible for articulating this *imperial* women's rights justification for war. Imperial feminism utilizes a masculinist militarism in drag. Imperial(ist) feminism obfuscates the use of gender decoys: women are both victims and perpetrators; constrained and yet free; neither exactly commander nor victim.

If rape and sexual humiliation are understood not as aberrations in war but as simply a form of war by other means, there is then a different context for seeing the disorder and chaos in Iraq that leaves many women barricaded in their homes. This is not simply about Islamic practices or Saddam Hussein's legacy, but rather about war itself. It also puts a different lens on the recent charges of sexual assault and rape by dozens of US servicewomen in the Persian Gulf area against their fellow soldiers.[68] It makes clear that gender degradation is integral to war and that war can therefore not be liberatory for women's rights.

The narratives of war take on more explicit gender trajectories today because the relation of sex to gender is in particular flux given this militarist stage of global capitalist patriarchy. It is in part why the most explicit conflict rages between patriarchal Islamic Osama extremists and global capitalist Bush patriarchs – they differ the most on the necessity of traditional patriarchal relations and their modernized versions. In the Balkan wars the raping of women was a central narrative demonizing Serb nationalism while the rape and sexual humiliation of Muslim male prisoners was largely silenced. More recently the sexual humiliation of Muslim men at Abu Ghraib largely silenced the sexual humiliation and violation of their women counterparts. Gender differentiation remains poignant in both narratives, while unsettling pre-existing sexual divides.

Today's militarist masculinism operates out of the enforced differentiation of woman from man – the 'othering' and differentiating of each through a hetero viewing of the self using white female decoys. The Iraq wars have finely tuned the dual role of imperial women – both as masculinized commanders and soldiers and as gender decoys. However, I also think that these silences of war *enforce* a disconnection and 'differentiation' between men and women that do not and cannot exist given the centrality of racialized/sexualized violence in war. This shared dehumanization also bespeaks the very opposite: men and women's shared humanity.

Sex and race combine and reformulate here. Bodies are disconnected from their gendered meaning. Brown men become like women of all colors, yet it is white women who supposedly dominate and hold the leashes – the white women who are also raped by their comrades in arms. This gendered chaos creates a new/old form of deception so that real people cannot be seen for their humanity. As such, the structures of power and domination defining the contours of their lives are put out of view.

Barbara Ehrenreich has argued that Abu Ghraib makes it clear that feminism – the idea that women need to be free to have the same rights as men – is an insufficient strategy. Fair enough; but this in part misreads Abu Ghraib. She writes that Abu Ghraib is a moment of "imperial arrogance, sexual depravity and gender equality".[69] But there is no gender equality to be seen here, just gender *depravity*, or at best a deformed equality that no one wishes for, and at this point, not even the women said to be equal. Most feminisms across the globe, and many at home, know that mimicking men is not equality or freedom.

Parallel issues are presented when Colin Powell and Condi Rice become the symbols for these wars. One should not presume that their presence means that racial and/or gender equality exists today for most black men and women. In reality, disproportionate numbers of blacks – men and women – are housed in US prisons; the same prisons that strip them naked and abuse them. What is really frightening is that Abu Ghraib can be made to look like feminism – but not a sort that I recognize. Abu Ghraib is hyper-imperialist masculinity run amok. Females are present to cover over the misogyny of building empire, while also actually building it.

So I think that there is little if anything to consider feminist here. Most women are in the military because of globalization and the restructuring of the labor force in the US and elsewhere. Jessica Lynch had applied for a job at Wal-Mart and when she did not get it, she decided to enlist. Lori Pies-tewa and Shoshanna Johnson, who both fought with Lynch, were single mothers looking to get an education. The three women charged over the crimes at Abu Ghraib are all working class. I see *necessity*, not equality here.

I want to be careful not to oversimplify the variety and differences that exist among soldiers in this war – especially, in this case, women. Johnson, a black woman soldier-cook, was shot and taken as a prisoner-of-war and then was rescued to return home to her young daughter. She says when she is asked about Lynndie England on the *Larry King Show*: there is no way I would ever wrap a rope around someone's neck and drag them around naked. They could court-martial me, or do anything else they wanted to punish me. I wouldn't do it. She also said that no soldier should ever follow an inhumane order. She also says that once captured she feared for her safety and the possibility of rape, but that after an early beating on the battlefield, she was always treated with respect. According to Jessica Lynch she also was treated with care and concern as a prisoner.[70] Despite her wrecked body, she refuses to demonize Iraq or become a voice for this war.

Women are used in the Abu Ghraib pictorial narrative to protect a heterosexist normativity. We see females abusing men, which protects sexual hierarchy and opposition but in reverse; don't ask don't tell is the rule of law here. These low-ranking women are clearly not in control of much of anything; they are a type of pawn supporting disgusting practices that they should have refused to perform. Their actions do not bespeak their own power or privilege yet they display the imperial power of white women over Muslim men. They are acting in a heterosexist hierarchical and punishing system of power. This same system of power now offers them up as cannon fodder. The complex web of sex, race, gender and class is woven deceptively and yet with consequence at Abu Ghraib. It is truly significant that Fast and Karpinski are white and that we do not see black women in these positions of command or implicated in sexual crimes like England. Because of the twisted effects of racialized sexuality, Johnson resonates differently as gender decoy.[71]

It is not insignificant that people in the US – men and women alike – were horrified to see women degrading prisoners at Abu Ghraib. Some of us even hoped that women were above this kind of action. Obviously, simple essentialism – that women are more mothering or caring or peaceful – is not simply true. Neither is it simply true that given many women's lives and their parental responsibilities they are as prone to war as most men. Women and men respond to the forces upon them and are constructed from them. Neither gender essentialism nor constructionism simply clarifies war. So, yes, Abu Ghraib bespeaks a larger problem than a few loose cannons deciding to abuse and torture prisoners. The obscene practices of human degradation were already in place in Afghanistan, and in our prisons at home in the US. It has now been revealed that former prison guards with records of abuse were interrogators of detainees at Guantanamo, and officials from the Afghan war instructed the military personnel at Abu Ghraib.

The problem is not just about the role that Defense Secretary Rumsfeld, Security Advisor Condoleezza Rice, Undersecretary of Defense and Intelligence Stephen Cambone and the commander of the detention center at Guantanamo, Geoffrey Miller, played. It is also about the larger system of racialized hetero-masculinity that is put in high gear at this moment of unilateral militarization. This structural system of hierarchical privilege and power 'others' anyone who is not in the business of empire building. There are few if any civilians left in these moments. Gendered/racialized individuals are never what they simply seem.

Because gender is so flexible and complex it is a perfect foil for obfuscation. When Kofi Annan says, invest in the women in Africa and they will help solve the AIDS problem; when people depend on women in the US to mobilize in terms of their disproportionate peace-making commitments; when women in Afghanistan and Iraq provide significant leadership for real democratic struggle; when women more readily become suicide bombers; *and* when women in the US are mobilized out of economic necessity to fight the wars of/on terror, there is no easy clarification. Real commitments to gender equality will be misused and abused by those in power. Gender differentiation will be mobilized for war *and* peace. This is the ugly side of the rewired patriarchy of war capitalism. Bush's wars of/on terror mask its realpolitik – that of a racist capitalist misogyny operating in a variety of drag.

Abu Ghraib showed us that humanity and inhumanity come in all colors, sexes and genders. War readies you to kill, to be on guard always, to trust no one who is the enemy. War, then, almost always destroys the very sense of humanity that allows you to see yourself in another, to see your connection with another instead of their difference from you. Brutality reflects this process of seeing and then not seeing another's humanity. Looking at the emasculated Iraqi prisoners at Abu Ghraib – from a distance – forced people in the US to see war upfront. Most of us saw more than we wanted to: the US wars of/on terror are ugly and debased; the war in Iraq is failing; we are not so different than Saddam Hussein.

Gender construction is a process without end. To the extent that cyber technology both creates and reflects discourses about the body – and in particularly militarized forms – cyber-tech allows and nurtures this 'newest' aspect of decoy status. Bodies float freer from the original site today because of their invisible visibility – which cyber communications demand and allow. The disembodiment of sex and labor in cyber-relations nurtures these new relations between sex, race and gender. And with this changed economy, militarized lives and war itself changes.

Masculinity and femininity and their specific racialized meanings are then always in flux. Linda Burnham calls attention to the "sexualization of national conquest" at Abu Ghraib and sees sexual domination as part of a "militarist hyper-sexuality".[72] This hyper-sexual moment is revealed because sexualized racism is always brought to the fore when systems of power are in crisis and too much of the truth of war is uncovered.

Unilateral power is blinded by a complete and total arrogance. The Bush administration thinks it is above the law, out of reach of any kind of accountability. Torture is OK. No one is innocent. The US military will police itself. It is its own court of last resort. There are no protections for prisoners. The war of/on terror terrorizes all who come in contact with it. The lines between combatant and civilian, rights and degradation, and white, black and brown men and women are realigned and remade. But this racialized gender flux takes place within the structural constraints of racialized patriarchy, and hetero-masculinized gender.

Tony Blair is emasculated as brown men capture the CARE worker Margaret Hassan and then murder her. And powerful nations stand helpless as foreign workers are rounded up and beheaded. Ultimatums are delivered and ignored and innocent people die. Race and gender appear emptied and terror-filled simultaneously. Masculinist warriors on both sides take no hostages.

The naked bodies of tortured Muslim men alongside white women holding cigarettes and leashes, and the absence and silencing of Muslim women at Abu Ghraib is a heart-rending reminder that war is unbearable. It would be a double heartbreak to think that people in the US abide any part of the violations at Abu Ghraib, especially in the name of feminism.

Notes

1 Gabriel Kolko, *Century of War* (New York: New Press, 1994), p. 111.
2 Kenn Baker, "We're in the Army Now", *Harper's*, vol. 307, no. 1841 (October 2003), pp. 35–46.
3 Angela Davis, *Are Prisons Obsolete?* (New York: Seven Stories Press, 2003), pp. 88, 92.

4 Ibid., pp. 24, 27.
5 Clive Thompson, "The Making of a Box Warrior", *New York Times Magazine*, August 23, 2004, pp. 33–7.
6 Jim Defede, "Mining the Matrix", *Mother Jones*, September/October 2004, p. 24.
7 Cynthia Enloe, *Maneuvers: The International Politics of Militarizing Women's Lives* (Berkeley: University of California Press, 2000), pp. 3, 4.
8 Ibid., pp. xii, 45.
9 Lory Manning, "Military Women", *Women's Review of Books*, vol. xxi, no. 5 (February 2004), p. 7.
10 Cynthia Enloe, *Maneuvers*, pp. xi, 280, 281.
11 Carol Burke, "One of the Boys", *Women's Review of Books*, vol. 23, Issue 2 (March/April, 2006), p. 3.
12 Rita Manchanda, "Maoist Insurgency in Nepal: Radicalizing Gendered Narratives", *Cultural Dynamics*, vol. 16, no. 2/3 (October 2004), pp. 237, 238, 245.
13 Brenda Moore, *Serving Our Country* (New Brunswick: Rutgers University Press, 2003), pp. xi, xii, 1, 3, 22, 30.
14 Ibid., pp. 130–3, 134.
15 D'Ann Campbell, "Women in Combat", *Journal of Military History*, vol. 57 (April 1993), pp. 301–23.
16 For an important discussion of gender configurations in the military, see Mary Fainsod Katzenstein, *Faithful and Fearless, Moving Feminist Protest Inside the Church and the Military* (Princeton: Princeton University Press, 1998).
17 Jeffrey Gettleman, "US Detains Iraqis, and Families Plead for News", *New York Times*, March 7, 2004, p. A1.
18 Cynthia Enloe, *Does Khaki Become You?* (Boston: South End Press, 1983).
19 Carol Burke, "Why They Love to Hate Her", *The Nation*, vol. 278, no. 11 (March 22, 2004), pp. 14.
20 Catherine Lutz, "Living Room Terrorists", *Women's Review of Books*, vol. xxi, no. 5 (February 2004), p. 17.
21 Monica Davey, "At Fort Riley Soldiers Just Back from Iraq Get Basic Training in Resuming Life", *New York Times*, May 31, 2004, p. A1.
22 Christopher Hedges, *War Is a Force That Gives Us Meaning* (New York: Public Affairs, 2002), pp. 3, 158, 171.
23 Lynda Boose, "TechnoMuscularity and the 'Boy Eternal'", in Amy Kaplan and Donald Pease, eds., *Cultures of US Imperialism* (Durham: Duke University Press, 1993), pp. 504, 605.
24 Sara Ruddick, "Notes Toward a Feminist Peace Politics", in Miriam Cooke and Angela Woollacott, eds., *Gendering War Talk* (Princeton: Princeton University Press, 1993), p. 291.
25 Klaus Theweleit, "The Bombs, Wombs and the Genders of War", in Cooke and Woollacott, eds., *Gendering War Talk*, p. 284.

26   Charlotte Hooper, *Manly States: Masculinities, International Relations and Gender Politics* (New York: Columbia University Press, 2001), pp. 76, 95.

27   Michael Sallah and Mitch Weiss, 'Buried Secrets, Brutal Truths', *The Blade*, May 12, 2003, p. 45.

28   Svetlana Alexievich, *Zinky Boys: Soviet Voices from the Afghanistan War* (New York: Norton, 1990), p. ix.

29   Margaret Higonnet, "Not So Quiet in No-Woman's-Land", in Cooke and Woollacott, eds., *Gendering War Talk*, pp. 205–26.

30   *Winter Soldier*, 20/20 Production, PO Box 198, New Hampshire.

31   Susan Jeffords, *The Remasculinization of America: Gender and the Vietnam War* (Bloomington: Indiana University Press, 1989), pp. xiv, 5, 168.

32   Carol Cohn, "Wars, Wimps and Women: Talking Gender and Thinking War", in Miriam Cooke and Angela Woollacott, eds., *Gendering War Talk*, pp. 228, 232.

33   Rick Bragg, *I Am a Soldier, Too: The Jessica Lynch Story* (New York: Alfred Knopf, 2003), p. 124.

34   Gillian Youngs, "Private Pain/Public Peace: Women's Rights as Human Rights and the Amnesty International Report on Violence against Women", *Signs*, vol. 28, no. 4 (Summer, 2003), p. 1209.

35   Beverly Allen, *Rape Warfare: The Hidden Genocide in Bosnia-Herzegovina and Croatia* (Minneapolis: University of Minnesota Press, 1996), pp. xii, 47, 62.

36   Susan McKay and Dyan Mazurana, *Where Are the Girls?* (Montreal: Rights and Democracy, 2004), p. 45.

37   Alexandra Stiglmayer, ed., *Mass Rape: The War against Women in Bosnia-Herzegovina* (Lincoln: University of Nebraska, 1992); and Zillah Eisenstein, *Hatreds: Racialized and Sexualized Conflicts of the 21st Century* (New York: Routledge, 1996).

38   Eve Ensler, "The New Paradigm: We Hold Within", in Medea Benjamin and Jodie Evans, eds. *Stop the Next War Now* (San Francisco: Inner Ocean Publishing, 2005), p. 28.

39   Yvette Abrams, presentation on "Feminist Identities and Global Struggles", at the *Future of Minority Studies Conference,* National Summer Institute, Cornell University, August 1, 2005.

40   Salman Masood, "Pakistani Leader's Comments on Rape Stir Outrage", *New York Times*, September 24, 2005, p. A3.

41   Eric Schmitt, "Military Women Reporting Rapes by US Soldiers", *New York Times*, February 26, 2004, p. A1.

42   Richard Rayner, "Women in the Warrior Culture", *New York Times Magazine*, June 22, 1997, pp. 24–55.

43   Amy Herdy and Miles Moffeit, "Camouflaging Criminals: Sexual Violence against Women in the Military", *Amnesty International Report*, vol. 30, no.1 (Spring, 2004), p. 23.

44   Rick Bragg, *I Am a Soldier, Too*, p. 95.

45 Lory Manning, "Military Women", p. 7.

46 Barbara Victor, *Army of Roses: Inside the World of Palestinian Women Suicide Bombers* (New York: St Martin's Press, 2003), pp. ix, 35, 7, 16.

47 Ibid., pp. 8, xi.

48 Jacqueline Rose, "Deadly Embrace", *London Review of Books*, vol. 26, 2005. Available at *www.lrb.co.uk/v26/h21/rose01.html*.

49 Steven Lee Myers, "Female Suicide Bombers Unnerve Russians", *New York Times*, May 24, 2003, p. A6.

50 Steven Lee Meyers, "From Dismal Chechnya, Women Turn to Bombs", *New York Times*, September 10, 2004, p. A1.

51 Terry Eagleton, "A Different Way of Death", *Guardian*, January 26, 2005, p. 5.

52 Vernon Lock, "Combat Heroine", *Washington Post*, November 23, 2003, p. D01. (www.washingtonpost.com)

53 Ira Berkow, "A Star Athlete, a Soldier, a Challenge", *New York Times*, June 3, 2004, p. A17.

54 Somini Sengupta, "For Iraqi Girls, Changing Land Narrows Lives", *New York Times*, June 27, 2004, p. A1.

55 Anthony Lewis, "Making Torture Legal", *New York Review of Books*, vol. LI, no. 12 (February 10, 2003), pp. 4–8.

56 David S. Cloud, "Private Found Guilty in Abu Ghraib Abuse", *New York Times*, September 27, 2005, p. A12.

57 As quoted in the Dateline interview, "Behind the Abu Ghraib Photos: An Exclusive Interview", October 2, 2005.

58 Kate Zernike, "Plea Deal Is Set for GI Pictured in Abuses in Iraq", *New York Times*, April 30, 2005, p. A1.

59 Janet Karpinski with Steven Strasser, *One Woman's Army* (New York: Miramax Books, 2005), pp. 48, 79, 81, 214, 221.

60 Marjorie Cohn, "Military Hides Cause of Women Soldiers' Deaths", TRUTHOUT/report, Monday January 30, 2006 at: *www.truthout.org/docs2006/013006J.shtml*.

61 Viveca Novak and Douglas Waller, "New Abuse Charges", *Time Magazine*, June 20, 2004, p. 23.

62 Alexander Cockburn, "Green Lights for Torture", *The Nation*, vol. 278, no. 21 (May 31, 2004), p. 9.

63 I am indebted to Susan Buck-Morss for this discussion. See Vera Proskurina, "Catherine the Great: translatio imperii and Translation of Gender", Davis Center, Harvard University: *www.aatseel.org/program/aatseel/2002/abstracts/Proskurina.ht*.

64 David D. Kirkpatrick, "Bush Judicial Nominee Nears Confirmation", *New York Times*, June 8, 2005, p. A14.

65 Thom Shanker, "Military Bill Backtracks on Women", *New York Times*, May 24, 2005, p. A24.

66   Thom Shanker, "House Bill Would Preserve and Limit, the Role of Women in Combat Zones", *New York Times*, May 20, 2005, p. A20.

67   For an important discussion of the political context defining this discussion see: Rosalind Petchesky "Phantom Towers: Feminist Reflections on the Battle Between Global Capital and Fundamentalist Terrorism", in Susan Hawthorne and Bronwyn Winter, *September 11, 2001, Feminist Perspectives* (North Melbourne, Australia: Spinifex, 2002), pp. 316–30.

68   Eric Schmitt, "Military Women Reporting Rapes by US Soldiers", *New York Times*, February 26, 2004, p. A1.

69   Barbara Ehrenreich, "What Abu Ghraib Taught Me", *www.Alternet.org/story*. May 20, 2004.

70   Rick Bragg, *I Am A Soldier Too*.

71   I am particularly indebted to comments from Rosalind Petchesky for clarification of this discussion.

72   Linda Burnham, "Sexual Domination in Uniform: An American Value" *War Times, www.war-times.org*, May 19, 2004.

3

Terrorized and Privatized Democracy

By January 2006 the US public is finally disenchanted with the war in Iraq, troubled by Bush's rationale for the use of torture, and disturbed by the news that his administration has used wiretaps to illegally monitor communications. It is clear that civil liberties have been gravely compromised at home and abroad. Over thirty-five career diplomats, economic advisors, National Security Council members, CIA staffers, and Army colonels have resigned over these issues. Nevertheless, our President continues to speak on behalf of democracy and freedom to the world, and extends these rights only to those who applaud him. He criticizes those who question his policies and tells them that they are giving comfort to the enemy. As such, he silences and criminalizes dissent.

It is amazing to me to see how anti-democratic practices can be couched in the language of democracy. So bombs are dropped, and people are detained and tortured abroad, while others are rounded up on our own streets to be deported or held in legal limbo. Given these moves towards a total power grab, I am left with my inadequate and incomplete language which queries imperial democracy for its neoliberal fascistic tendencies. Civil rights are denuded and the rule of liberal democratic law is officially under assault, even if this reality has not arrived for most Americans yet. At this juncture of global capitalism the fascistic imperial side of democracy is increasingly located at home, inside the US, and more readily exposed at its extremities.

Even Alberto J. Mora, former General Counsel of the US Navy, a respected conservative who admired Ronald Reagan, who served in the first and second Bush administrations, supported the 'war on terror' and the invasion of Iraq, appears to agree at least in part with the above assessment. Starting as early as December 2002, Mora voiced his concern and resistance to the detainee abuse in Iraq and Guantanamo as it was being uncovered. He wrote in memos that cruelty is unlawful, that personal dignity is a human constitutional right, and that "unlawful enemy combatants" must and do have these rights. "If you make this exception, the whole constitution crumbles. It is a transformative issue."[1] He is sickened and disheartened by these anti-democratic moves by the Bush administration.

The contradictions of this politics of imperial democracy in flux abound. Bush demands that Americans live in an 'ownership society' – one where people depend on themselves rather than others. Meanwhile he creates the largest deficit in history and his corporate friends get richer. He uses privatization – the privileging of business over government – as his guide and denudes the public sphere of its social responsibilities. The more privatized and imperial the country, the less equal and less just. And the less just, the more militarist it must become. Hence the significance of the wars of/on terror that underpin these moves.

Terrorism is the new communism. Many of the same terror networks that the US supported and depended upon to fight the Soviet Union in Afghanistan, Iraq and Iran have now become the newest enemy. Friend and foe twist and turn. It is particularly significant that the bad Muslims of today are the good Muslims of the Cold War period.[2]

Global capitalism now dominates in singular fashion. This has necessitated and revealed the business of war and its corporatization in newer form. As war becomes more privatized and businesslike, the less regulated and accountable it becomes. As such, the more privatized war is, the more big business comes to shape war directly, making it ever less regulated and ever less accountable. It follows, then, that the more corporate, the less accountable and the less democratic *and* the more secrecy, deception, and torture there is. It is why even many in the military take umbrage at the new moves towards unaccountable power.

The corporate power grab of the Iraq war alongside a trillion-dollar debt construct an unstable political and economic climate for the US along with the globe. Anti-terror rhetoric is used to justify these circumstances, while US wars are disproportionately fought by men and women of color. As such, war capitalism is an incredible site of both cover-up and exposure. It is cloaked in the diverse racial/ethnic and gender make-up of fighting forces themselves so that the excessive and concentrated display of power is presented in dispersed fashion along racial and sexual lines. Meanwhile, heterosexist gender hierarchy is protected by disciplining gays.

Bush's right-wing market fanaticism has become more and more disconnected from liberal democratic discourse. The talk and promise of racial and sexual equality and social and political justice have been abandoned because of their supposed success, and displaced by imperial democracy's focus on fear. The wars of/on terror terrorize people and smash the possibility for seeing a shared sense of humanity.

When I started to read the early reports about US treatment of detainees and prisoners in Afghanistan, and Guantanamo, and Iraq I could not sleep.

Terrorism, torture and the new extremism

Jean Baudrillard writes that the US was humiliated on September 11, 2001; that global power was symbolically defeated on that day; and that terrorism is "our own judgment and penalty".[3] The humiliation was emasculating so war was the answer. The war on terror was the perfect foil: no boundaries, no specific site, no end to it in sight. The standoff with Saddam Hussein over Iraq's alleged weapons of mass destruction (WMD) stood in place of a focused and proven agenda.[4] National security became the central focus; surveillance and discipline trumped everything, especially civil rights. The Patriot Act promised to secure domestic safety but this was in exchange for lessening personal privacy, increasing government secrecy, increasing surveillance of immigrants, initiating new guidelines for monitoring suspicious individuals, and new death penalties. Security is positioned against rights, and "terror-pork" replaces needed public policies.[5] The war was now against civil rights and its laws.

The US occupation of Iraq and Afghanistan creates new forms of terror and new dissidents and insurgents. The extremist insurgents who capture and kill foreigners, be they Americans, Germans, Japanese, Chinese, Pakistanis, spiral the war further out of control. Terror tactics on all sides initiate new networks that exist across geographical boundaries, much like global capital and its transnational technologies. The militarization of the globe becomes an integral part of its market privatization.

Former US Treasury Secretary Paul O'Neill rejected Bush's market extremism by resigning. He viewed Bush's tax policies as a major threat to national security. O'Neill deeply believed that privatization and deregulation were so out of control that he could no longer support the final tax cut package for the richest Americans. He, along with many centrist capitalists, thinks Bush's policies undermine the very stability of the system of capitalism itself. After the Enron scandal O'Neill pushed for more accountability of CEOs but no one in the administration was interested.[6] Instead, the administration continued to herald the idea of an "ownership" society – more privatization policies would be initiated in order to encourage people's responsibility for their own lives – to replace the expectation that there should be governmental/public support or assistance. An early initiative launched by Bush was to privatize social security – for people to look less to government and more to themselves. This has come to nothing.

Bush's "ownership" society is one that privileges the private aspects of all forms of property. It is why there are currently such keen debates about the meaning of intellectual property, and fair use, and the protection of copyright. New digital technologies undermine some of these earlier notions of private ownership. File sharing and remixing are found to be illegal by this earlier standard of property rights.[7] Meanwhile, Paul Krugman writes that savage cuts are made to education, health care, veterans' benefits and environmental protection to help with the deficit – reducing it by one sixth – when a cut in tax rates for the high income brackets would greatly more efficiently reduce the deficit – by one third.[8]

O'Neill argues for what he sees as an ethical and not an extremist capitalism. Much like George Soros, he thinks economic extremism undermines liberal democracy, and that it is in the interest of the US to do its share to deal with global warming and AIDS in Africa. Richard Clarke, as former counter-terrorist chief, agrees in kind about economic and political extremism. He writes that the extremist rhetoric used in the war on Iraq has simply created more, not less terror. He says the "administration has squandered the opportunity to eliminate Al Qaeda and instead strengthened our enemies by going off on a completely unnecessary tangent, the invasion of Iraq". Given our bad policies based on bad facts he says that Al Qaeda has emerged in much stronger and tougher form.[9] But this is not what the Bush extremists – Richard Perle, Paul Wolfowitz, Dick Cheney, and John Ashcroft – see as true.

And the issue of facts is key here. The Bush administration ignores, deceives, and lies on multiple fronts. George Tenet, former director of the CIA, made clear before resigning that the WMDs alleged to exist in Iraq were never an "imminent threat".[10] The overstated claims about WMDs are part of a pattern of repeated deceit. Although numerous scientists write that climate change is a major problem for national security, the Bush administration continues to support oil and gas interests rather than challenge the carbon dioxide emissions that propel global warming. The administration simply ignores and/or doctors the data.[11] As a result it became quite ordinary to distort scientific facts and mislead the public for partisan political ends. The Bush White House "purges, censors and black-lists" scientists' and engineers' research findings that question and under-mine "the profits of the Administration's corporate backers".[12] Scientists who work on behalf of the environment, arms control and the public health say their findings are ignored and falsified and that reports are censored and suppressed.[13]

This deception and distortion underpin the extremist politics of the Bush administration – from the detainees at Guantanamo Bay to Halliburton's war profits to the 2004 report on minority health that was revised to enhance and improve the data. The Bush administration admits "improperly altering" the racial and ethnic disparities in health care and has promised to provide an "unexpurgated document".[14] This kind of lying and deceit is usually identified with fascistic and/or totalitarian regimes; yet it is becoming integral to US imperial neoliberal democracy.

Bush is becoming more unaccountable, arrogant, and corrupt as he uses deception to achieve his political agenda. This kind of excessive dema-goguery articulates a particular strand of political extremism that allows corporate excesses like the thievery by Enron's CEOs. Such market extremism leaves many centrist Republicans and neoliberals running for cover from Bush's Christian/market fundamentalism.[15]

Continual moves to authorize torture as a form of needed interrogation document the rightward drift towards fascistic democracy. Alberto Gonzales argues that the CIA falls outside the parameters demanding humane treatment of prisoners. He also believes that the international prohibition against unusual and inhumane treatment has a "limited read" and does not apply in all cases to "aliens overseas". As Attorney General he says that the administration does not support torture but endorses the use of extreme interrogation.[16] Mark Danner writes that once Gonzales was confirmed as Attorney General, torture belonged to all of us.[17]

Documenting democracy's demise

Terror creates and sustains excessive and extremist politics, as is seen in White House memos on torture. Human Rights Watch documents the continual circumvention of law in the treatment of prisoners and detainees in Afghanistan, at Guantanamo, and in Abu Ghraib. Reed Brody writes that the Bush administration has "eviscerated the important protections" of the Geneva Convention of 1949. Humiliation and degradation as well as coercive interrogation are now permissible; the Commander-in-Chief is not bound by international laws; offshore and undisclosed and off-limits sites are created in which to detain terror suspects.

Afghan prisoners were named "detainees" so that they would not qualify for the protections of the Geneva Conventions. They were designated "nobodies", as not soldiers. This naming of prisoners authorized the pain and suffering and severe humiliation of detainees. Donald Rumsfeld initiated these practices in order to "exploit internees for actionable intelligence".[18] He believes that terrorists are a difficult and new breed of enemy that require new ways to garner information. This unconventional war needs unconventional and, obviously, undemocratic practices.

The Bush administration has determined that the wars of/on terror can only be fought effectively with new rules, ones that are less constraining and protective of prisoner rights. The new practices need to allow for stress and duress but should not include severe beatings, burning with cigarettes, electric shocks to the genitals, rape or sexual assault. This extreme form of interrogation – which the Bush administration refuses to call torture – "may be justified" in the war on terror in order to gain needed intelligence. The definition of torture needs to be clarified and limited to "acts that are specifically intended to inflict severe physical or mental pain and suffering that is hard to endure". As formulated by Assistant Attorney General Jay S. Bybee in an August 2002 Justice Department memo for the White House, there must be specific intent to do harm. And pain must lead to organ failure, impairment of bodily function, or death.[19]

Many of the seven hundred detainees from forty-four different countries exist at sites beyond the reach of jurisdiction by US courts.[20] It is thought that there are dozens of 'ghost detainees' – prisoners who are kept off the prison rolls – who have disappeared to undisclosed locations. Approximately one dozen Al Qaeda operatives are said to have disappeared in US custody.[21] Shaming – sexually degrading men and women through nudity – has become a practice of choice. Shackling and hypothermia have become common.

The new interrogation rules – established at Bagram detention center in Afghanistan where two prisoners died in incidents determined to be homicides – were also posted on a wall at Abu Ghraib. The Human Rights

Watch Report cites General Antonio Taguba's findings: "numerous incidents of sadistic, blatant, and wanton criminal abuses" were inflicted on detainees at Abu Ghraib. And since Bush declared an end to major combat in Iraq, more than 12,000 Iraqis have been taken into custody by US forces. It is thought that 70 to 90 percent of those in custody in Iraq in 2003 were arrested by mistake.[22]

Despite the recognition of horrific wrongdoing at Abu Ghraib by an Independent Panel chaired by James Schlesinger to review DOD (Department of Defense) detention operations, little accountability has been rendered. The report starts: "The events of October through December 2003 in the night shift of Tier 1 at Abu Ghraib prison were acts of brutality and purposeless sadism." Yet the rest of the report simply calls this "deviant behavior" and says it was "not a part of authorized interrogations". The aberrant behavior was explained as resulting from "confusing and inconsistent interrogation technique policies", overcrowding, underresourcing, understaffing, and extreme duress for the US troops. It is an interesting aside that the report notes that "relevant army manuals and publications were available only on-line, but personnel did not have access to computers or the Internet". The report concludes that the global war on terror (GWOT) involves "new conditions and new threats. Doctrine must be adjusted accordingly."[23]

Investigations into activity at Abu Ghraib repeatedly argue that a lack of resources, manpower, and equipment played a role in the abuses. Karpinski writes that the number of detainees continued to rise without enough military police to do the job and that conditions went from bad to worse. As the war continued despite Bush's declaration of its end, and the number of detainees swelled to 5,000 in the fall of 2003, interrogation became more brutal. Although there is a torture trail leading to Abu Ghraib, most government-sponsored reports argue that the events at Abu Ghraib were the exception to the rule. Lack of training and oversight and an absence of leadership are repeatedly noted as cause for concern leading to faulty "intelligence architecture". War doctrine is not faulted here but rather a need for "communication equipment, computers and sufficient bandwith, access to data bases and the fusion and collaboration of intelligence data" is noted.[24]

The notion of a digital war and its new needs are key to this moment. Donald Rumsfeld took charge of modernizing the military – downsizing and restructuring it to be lean and mean. This process followed the downsizing and restructuring of the social welfare state and the notion of head. No surprise that Judy Steinberg, Dean's wife and a doctor, was pathologized as well. She was just too ordinary: like most women, too busy with her job to campaign. Patriarchy runs deep here; and the actual biological sex of the body does not tell the whole story. Bush stands before us and says 'bring 'em on'. Frank Rich sums up the lunacy: "Only in an election year ruled by fiction could a sissy who used daddy's connections to escape Vietnam turn an actual war hero into a girlie man."[16]

Then Reagan died and the whole country was asked to mourn as though he was a great man and president. We are asked to not remember that he is/was responsible for enabling the very terror networks of today in his Cold War policies against the Soviets. His policies nurtured the most extremist factions of Islamic countries, especially in the Afghan war with the Soviets. Yet it appeared like the entire country was in mourning: wanting to embrace a leader who seemed more in charge.

I remember how inept Reagan was, an actor, a pretender-in-chief. In the official script Nancy Reagan remains the perfect, dutiful wife. We are told that theirs was a true love story. That they lived for each other, idolized each other. That she spent the last ten years of her life caring for him in adoring fashion. Alzheimer's claimed Reagan's life and this truly is a very sad story. But this story is taken over to tell another – the story of how women, gendered as wives, shall remain loyal and devoted. Never mind that it helps to be rich with millions to spare.

Gay marriage and gender fluidity

Marriage and family, and therefore masculinist privilege located here, are in flux. The traditional family and its gender constructs remain both static and changing. Marriage authorizes, institutionalizes, and codifies the meanings and relations of gender: man and woman, husband and wife. Despite Bush's right-wing right-to-lifers and their glorification of 'family values', only one quarter of households in the US now include two parents and their children. About one third of women in the US are single today, and many of them are now choosing to bear and raise children alone. The multiplicity of gender choices is creating an institutional crisis for marriage. Fewer people marry, people marry later, and half of all marriages end in divorce. Obviously, marriage needs all the assist it can muster.

It is more than interesting that in the midst of the heightened militarization of the US and the war in Iraq, gay marriage promises to continue to be a major challenge to traditional notions of patriarchal heterosexual marriage. Its legalization in Massachusetts in 2005 was just the beginning of this process. Yet the military remains a last bastion of homophobia where it remains legal to discriminate against homosexuals. One might remember that Bill Clinton early on in his presidency tried to change the military's anti-gay regulations. He quickly reversed course when challenged by right-wing Republicans, leaving the policy as one of: don't ask, don't tell.

A decade later, gay marriage is on the political agenda. Gays want and need the same rights as heterosexuals when it comes to health care insurance, life proxies, rights to children, et cetera.[17] Yet I sometimes wonder why gays would want to board a sinking ship. Sinking or not, gays want the legal standing of the family, and the rights it articulates for those who occupy its space. I cannot help but wonder again: maybe it is that gays have demonstrated alternative family relationships that work and heterosexuals have followed their lead by choosing not to marry. Get the gays on board with marriage, and get heterosexuals back on track.

At issue is the place of sex in relation to the gendered relations of family and marriage. If marriage can sustain itself in patriarchal form without heterosexism, then maybe so can the military. Although gay marriage seems to be a progressive, democratizing move towards a more encompassing notion of civil rights, it is also possibly not that. Gay marriage just might be another aspect of militarization in another guise. Marriage will regulate and discipline gays' lives as it does the lives of heterosexuals. And the imperial state will invade the bedroom from a new entry port.

There are some similarities to the decoy status of women's rights discourse in this instance. Assimilation is not the same thing as liberation. "Equality for queers inevitably means equal rights on straight terms."[18] Rights discourse presumes an unequal structure to begin with although it demands an equality – meaning sameness – that can be destabilizing of established privilege. At this point in time it remains to be seen if gay marriage will be an accommodation, or a subversion. Imperial democracy is incredibly adept at appropriating rights and calling it democracy.

It is significant, if not remarkable, that issues of gay rights keep bursting forward. Even Vice-President Cheney was forced to publicly recognize that his daughter Maureen is gay. She directed his 2004 campaign. Both he and Lynne act protective of their family and daughter although neither has ever spoken publicly against the President's homophobic administration. Dick got testy with both John Kerry and John Edwards for bringing up the issue of his gay daughter in the election, as though he wants to forget about it, and as though they are playing dirty. Maureen was not 'outed'; but in some sense Dick, as the father, and Republicans, as his party, were. The politics of sexuality continues to spill out as imperial democracy militarizes and represses itself.

Despite everything, same-sex marriage became a wedge issue in some states in the 2004 election. Proposed state constitutional amendments banning same-sex marriage are said to have increased the conservative voter turnout in the states with such proposed amendments.[19] Here we see imperial heterosexist repression successfully in action.

Bush's cowgirls

Laura Flanders speaks of the Bush women as "an extremist administration's female front". Bush's cabinet originally had five women; only one had children, two were unmarried, and two were in childless marriages. Interesting data.[20] Early on in the presidency, Laura Bush was very much the traditional wife and mother, although we saw little of her with her daughters. She was the enabler in chief of her recovering alcoholic husband and his two daughters who struggle with their own drinking problems. By his second administration, Laura becomes an activist, traveling outside the country on behalf of women's rights. She tries to make her husband look kinder and gentler while he wages war. She embodies gender fluidity, as did Hillary Clinton as first lady and then as New York senator. Interestingly, Hillary became more manly and aggressive as Bill became more humiliated and womanly. Laura has become more acute as her husband becomes more inept.

Bush's cowgirls orchestrate his wartime strategies. They live a life that is beholden to earlier struggles for sexual equality and civil rights, while they disclaim connection to these movements. Condoleezza Rice says she has gotten where she is because she was brought up to depend on herself and work hard. At the same time she acknowledges the civil rights movement when she tries to gain acceptance for the continuance of the Iraq war. In these instances she readily uses the civil rights movement as proof of how hard it is to build democracy; that even the US had a long process of struggle to achieve democracy for all its citizens. And she offers herself as an example of the success of democracy. She speaks about her childhood, defined by racism, in Alabama to celebrate how far she and the US have come from all this. She nudges fledgling democracies to work hard, like we have, to make it work.

Even though one of the four girls killed in the bombing of the 16th Street Baptist Church years ago was her childhood friend, she lived in a protected bubble in Birmingham, Alabama. Although she says she looks forward to race-blind days, she seems divorced from the deep feelings of pain tied to racism.[21] She testified on behalf of the Bush administration at the 9/11 hearings and she acted brisk, rigid, precise, and unemotional. She has sacrificed family to be counted as a loyal player even if sometimes in neo-mammy form.

Condi Rice, like lots of rich white girls, was an incredible classical piano player in her youth. She later becomes a Soviet specialist although she never saw the Soviet collapse coming. She was a provost at Stanford University and oversaw the decline of affirmative action hiring. She served on the National Security Council during Bush senior's administration and became a board member of Chevron. After 9/11 she is criticized for ignoring crucial information about Al Qaeda as National Security Advisor. Even so, she was promoted to Secretary of State. She uses her black gendered skin to authorize and legitimize a politics of extreme war. And then she turns around and says she prefers Republicans because they treat her as an individual, not as a member of a racial group, or any other kind of group. Her gender and race are in play here at the same time that they are continually misidentified.

As a black woman Condi Rice has different options than the other white Bush cowgirls. Most of them are married; several have children. She instead remains a single woman. Even though almost every picture of her views her long slender legs, there is no man (or woman) in her life, just George W. She assumes a presence often as a little girl; what Patricia Williams has called a "racialized prurient prudishness".[22] This allows her to occupy a space close to the President without creating racial or sexual discomfort; she remains either the child, or the mammy, and he the father or the son. She is called the warrior princess and replaced Colin Powell, who is deemed too much of a girlie-man. Maureen Dowd calls her a "bachelorette workaholic".[23]

But other times Condoleezza Rice depicts the gender multiplicity inherent in her decoy status. She wears high black boots, and coats that often sport military buttons and fashion, and she appears more dominatrix than prudish. Other times she is described as more diplomatic than militarist, and yet she continues to defend the newest forms of extreme interrogation without hesitancy.[24] She asserts that we are winning the war in Iraq and that democracy will triumph. A statement by her is read to the delegates at the "Bejing + 10 Commemoration"; it states that the US "is committed to working in partnerships with other nations to enlarge the freedom and empowerment of women".[25] At the same time Iraqi women's rights in the new constitution are gravely threatened in the name of Shari'a law.

Condi parlays her womanly status, and also denies it. The French received her and were said to be "charmed". She was referred to as "Chère Condi" in *Le Monde*. Headlines proclaim that Condi "attempts to seduce Paris" with her pumps, pearls and accessories.[26] Her classy style almost makes her white as she feminizes the new militarism with a variety of gender codings.

Comparisons are regularly drawn today between Condi and Hillary. Some have even speculated that they could run against each other in the 2008 presidential election. Their similarities range from their favorite designer – Oscar de la Renta – to their favorite Ferregamo shoes, to their love of power and their manipulations of gender politics. Both present a variety of genders, alongside their structural constraints. So they often are masculinized as stiff, and pert, and desexualized: Condi with no husband in sight so far and Hillary with a husband she no longer lives with full-time.

Condi and Hillary are more similar than they are different, and yet not quite the same. Hillary supports Condi's war. Hillary still had not renounced it in November 2005, even as others in Congress had begun to speak out critically. She denounces unwanted pregnancies and remains against gay marriage. She is described as moving toward the center and as carving a centrist position even though she has never been anything other than this, a neoliberal Democrat. She is asked by the Pentagon to join a select panel that is considering improving military readiness, and she ranks among the dozen most conservative Democrats in the Senate given her voting record.[27] Hillary is the perfect gender decoy. She is depicted as too liberal, too feminist, too critical of women who just make cookies. In the process she desexes gender while regendering sex.

Karen Hughes – Bush's closest female confidant – is very married. She *sort of* left the White House after the first administration in order to do better by her young son and husband. She describes the life of assistant to the President as fabulous, but too consuming. She opts for her mommy-

and-wife role, but not completely. She still continues to travel regularly to Washington to help craft the gentler, kinder, more compassionate Bush. She parlays her knowledge as a mom and woman to soften Bush's crass masculinism. Bush recognizes how important his moms are, chiding a senior official demanding early-morning meetings with: "Don't run off my mothers." Hughes uses her insights as a woman living inside patriarchal gender to articulate the imperial agenda. And she uses religion, and her belief in God, to authorize her stance. She thanks her Bible group at the start of her book, *Ten Minutes from Normal.*[28]

Hughes, as a neoliberal feminist using women's rights discourse to make war, spun the Afghan war as though it would liberate women. She writes: "I thought focusing on the plight of Afghan women and girls was a way to highlight the cruel nature of the people we were up against."[29] It is significant how Hughes *et al.* on the one hand choose to ignore the increased violence in Afghan women's lives today, and on the other hand use the violence to justify the continuation of war.

Hughes pretends to be normal: religious, married, and at home, focused on family. But she has never been simply "normal", by her own description. Yet she deploys this notion of normal to regulate and discipline women, in general. She normalizes her life of faith and family even though this flies in the face of her own choices, and the necessities of most women today. Only wealthy women can take care of their families without a paying job; and most women can never achieve the job she occupies anyway. But it is Hughes's job to militarize compassionately the discourses surrounding women's lives. When asked about the March for Women's Lives organized to protect women's reproductive rights, she responds: "I think after September 11th the American people are valuing life more and realizing we need policies to value the dignity and worth of every life." She continues, that such policies are needed as we face a terror network that devalues life, even the innocent and their own.[30] She militaristically likens both abortion and terrorism to the killing of innocents. Her anti-abortion stance becomes one with the wars of/on terror.

Hughes is an effective decoy. She says she loves Bush and is devoted to him. She uses her station to activate his agenda and loves the power bestowed upon her. Both he and she use her gender to soften and disguise the cruelty of his regime. Her gender democratizes her extremist politics because she seems like lots of women. She works hard. She loves her family. She thinks women are talented, maybe even more so than men. She likes to do sports and keep physically fit. She is torn by the demands of her life. She wants time to cook and do the things she enjoys. She has lots of energy. These traits that connect with the gendering of most women's lives democratize Hughes and allow her a disguise for politics in another form.

Hughes is the smooth-talking mom who makes war on Iraq and continually speaks against the terror of "killing innocents". She travels to Saudi Arabia on her goodwill mission in September 2005 thinking that everyone wants to be like Americans, especially like American women. So she was a bit caught off-guard when Saudi women – obstetricians and gynecologists – let her know that many of them happily chose the wearing of the abayya, the headcovering, that Hughes just considered problematic.[31] Hughes, who manipulates and parlays gender meanings on her own behalf, does not seem to recognize gender pluralism elsewhere. She was ill prepared to meet with Turkish women who made clear to her that so long as Iraq is under US occupation they cannot talk about cooperation between women in the US and Turkey. Hughes sees herself and the US as a savior, and these women in Egypt, Saudi Arabia and Turkey do not want to be saved by a neoliberal feminist politics of imperial domination. Imperial notions of gendering and gendered war stand in stark contrast to their countries' needs and their needs as females and women.

The gendering of politics is war in yet another form. Gender exists in recognizable forms and does not. So even Mary Matalin, former assistant to Vice-President Cheney, has taken a break to be a full-time mommy to her two daughters. She starts her book, "I only care about my daughters" and "there is no greater love than the love you have for your children".[32] She wants to slow down and put her family above all else.

She rails against feminism. Feminists want to *be* boys and men, and she just wants to be able to *do* the things boys and men can do. "I just wanted to have the same fun boys had." She is extremely critical of what she terms the victimology of feminism ... and the way feminists deny nature and the difference between men and women. "We're different from stem to stem ..." She embraces gggrrrl power for her daughters in imperial fashion, as though those who can will succeed.[33] She supports Bush's policies and his wars and I know her daughters will not have to fight them. They could maybe even grow up to be the President who makes more war.

Matalin's selfishness and insularity from within the family unit also articulate a neoliberal feminism. She is feminist in that she thinks the sky should be and is the limit for anyone, female or male. But she is neoliberal in her complete individualism and denial of constraints. I wonder whether she thinks abortion needs to be legal for her daughters, or if abstinence will be enough to protect them.

As I mentioned earlier, in late September 2005 the new TV show, *Commander-in-Chief* hit the air. Obviously someone thought that the US public is ready to think about a female president. It is a series that stars Geena Davis as MacKenzie Allen, the first US female president. The series simultaneously militarizes the presidency and resexes it. Davis became president, in the first show, by accident. She is vice-president when the president dies. The accidental nature of her presidency makes a female president real and not real. She was not actually elected so her femaleness is not completely destabilizing.

In the first show we see the elected president on his deathbed asking MacKenzie to step aside and let the Speaker of the House take over as next in line. He tells her it would not be fair for her to take office because she was picked as his vice-president so that he could get the woman's vote. He tells her that she does not share the president's politics, and is too liberal. She thinks about it, and almost decides to step aside. But then the Speaker meets with her and again tells her she had initially just been a piece of theatre and that the Islamic world will never take her or the US seriously, because she is just a woman. By now MacKenzie is insulted, as a woman. She does not like being treated like a bag of hormones – by either her home country or the Muslim world. She quietly but forcefully decides to become the next President of the US.

In the first place, it is a sign of the militarized times that the series is called *Commander-in-Chief*. The first episodes depict an imperial presidency in white female face. MacKenzie sends in the marines to rescue a poor, oppressed African woman threatened by Shari'a law with death for adultery. The president is tough on terrorists but says she won't countenance knowing of torture. She says that freedom is "our gift to the world". She is presented as a "wife, mother and leader". She tells the press not to "mess with her three kids". Her husband struggles unhappily with his 'first husband' status. There is much discussion of what to call him. I am sure lots of people watching the show are wondering about Bill Clinton. In the meantime sex and gender trump each other in confused forms.

Geena Davis plays the role of a president who is competent, strong, and also flexible and thoughtful. She negotiates and compromises, like a woman; and is steadfast and tough, like a man. The storylines are very closely aligned with the 'real' world and yet the politics is played out as TV soap opera. The lines of real and simulacra are fully blurred. TV is real, and nothing at all like reality. While other countries elect female presidents, we have one on TV. The series is canceled after a brief season.

Gendering gender in testosterone elections

All the women I know across the globe believe that they should have gotten to vote in the US 2004 election. They say they live with the consequences of Bush's policies so they should get to choose. And if the globe could have chosen, Bush would have lost.

Election signs read: "W" – from George Walker Bush – "stands for women". But "W" stands for war and world domination, not women. How can "W" stand for, or on behalf of, women when the Republican party thinks that the best way to put someone down is to call them a girlie-man? The masculinist stance of the Republican party is at an all-time arrogant high. As soon as John Edwards was picked as the vice-presidential candidate Bush quickly responded: I didn't pick my vice-president because he's a pretty face, but because he can do the job. The subtext here: we don't need a pretty face – like a woman or a fag – who can't get the job done.

Vice-President Dick Cheney mocked his vice-presidential rival at the Republican convention. The intended meaning: Democrats are like pretty girls, ineffective and waffling. Edwards is regendered as a pretty woman in order to negate him as manly – competent and strong, like a man. His gender becomes disembodied while his sex is regendered. Their whiteness silently constructs the racialized meanings here. The Republican convention rhetoric depicted the Democrats as an ineffectual party trying to make a kinder and more sensitive foreign policy, as though kindness makes you a wimp ... like a woman ... not manly ... not capable of being commander-in-chief; unable to fight a war on terror. The Republicans use gendered language to humiliate and undermine. Women are sissies, men rule. Democrats are like women. It is significant that this takes place when none of the presidential and vice-presidential candidates are even female.

This contemptuous tenor made it almost impossible to think and talk and be understood. This hyper-militarism uses women as gender decoys to confuse and mystify the realities of power. At the Republican convention the office of the president was reduced to the status of commander-in-chief ... the wars of/on terror silenced everything else that deeply matters. In a total inversion of the real, Bush, who refused to serve in the Vietnam War, was presented as the manlier man; and Kerry who actually fought is de-masculinized.

It is hard to believe that the phrase "'W' in George W. stands for women" was ever deployed in the first place. "W" does not stand for most women here. And it does not stand for most females in countries devastated by the imperial politics of the US wars of/on terror, or in the maquiladora factories, or in the Nike plants in El Salvador or Bangladesh, or China. But even more problematic is the way this phrase disassociates women from the rest of humanity, and genders them while doing so. Women and men are more similar than different and not different in the ways that masculinism says they are. Women and men, and males and females share common differences and different commonalities. But the "W" genders. It is meant to separate and discipline women from men.

Women are affected by Bush's policies – in ways like men, and then in specific ways as female. This doubled visor/vision cannot be seen from the standard of masculinism, because male privilege universalizes the site of gender from the site of manhood. Patriarchy establishes the male visor as the single site and excludes women and makes them invisible while doing so. Females must specify their own situation as part of the larger construct of womanhood along with racial and class identities. They are a part of a sexual class and a part of humanity simultaneously. Human rights and women's rights bespeak these different negotiations.

Bush's record on war, the environment, health care, jobs, et cetera is bad for almost all men and women. Men and women are dying in the Gulf. Men and women are coming back maimed from the Gulf. Men and women are incarcerated and suffering in our prisons. War is bad for all humans. Environmental destruction is bad for all humans. Cancer kills and devastates all humans. All humans need health care. All humans need a good education. All humans want a fair wage and a good job.

Tax cuts for the rich mean there is less for all the rest of us. A trillion-dollar war in Iraq means there is less for the necessities of life: our schools, our hospitals, our medical system, our monies for scientific research, our roads, and airports, and bridges. There is then less for everything else as well. The cost of the war in Iraq could cover health care for the 43 million people without any in the US. Instead we lack a public health program. People would be able to get the drugs they need. AIDS would be a different disease because its treatment would have a different orientation:

prevention rather than surveillance. We could have state-of-the-art public schools throughout the country, but do not. Our environment would not be self-destructing. We would not have to stop eating fish because the waters are contaminated.

All the above affects women in particular ways, and yet none are simply best understood as only women's issues. AIDS affects all people. We have an AIDS epidemic in our prisons and there is no program in place to distribute condoms. Condoms are an issue for men and women and they are needed in the prisons to stem the spread of AIDS inside and outside the prison. This is of particular note to black women because many black men are leaving prison infected.

AIDS is a world epidemic and the US refuses funds in Africa to programs that provide abortions to women with AIDS. Both here and abroad these policies are devastating to humanity as a whole and specifically to women, when black women in the US account for 70 percent of all new AIDS cases in the US last year. Stephen Lewis, former Canadian Ambassador to the UN and currently the UN special envoy for HIV / AIDS in Africa, states that for the past twenty years the numbers of infected women have grown exponentially in Africa. Now almost 50 percent of new cases worldwide are women, and in Africa the percentage is 59 percent rising to 75 percent for women aged 15–24 years old. These women die agonizing deaths and yet nothing is being done. Lewis says, "when the rights of women are involved, the world goes into reverse".[34] Bush's policies are killing black and African women while Condoleezza Rice hangs out at Camp David and advises Bush on national security.

Meanwhile, when Vice-President Cheney and John Edwards were asked in their election debate about the crisis levels of AIDS among African American women in the United States, neither one of them claimed to know anything about it. Even though black women are thirteen times more likely to die from AIDS than their white counterparts, neither candidate seemed troubled by their ignorance. I was thinking: how could they not know? How could they not apologize for not knowing? How could they think that this was not important enough to know?

Bush's AIDS policies fantasizing abstinence represent an extremist right-wing zealotry that is creating a health crisis across the globe. Most of the 15 billion dollars promised by Bush for Africa, in an early State of the Union address, has not been spent because the programs cannot pass the sexual litmus test of his administration. When I attended the World AIDS conference in Bangkok, 2004, there were signs everywhere asking Bush to lift the gag rule and distribute the funds that he had promised.

Abortion law and availability are in continuing jeopardy. In November 2004, Congress passed a $388 billion spending bill that allows health providers, including health insurers, public or private hospitals, clinics, and pharmacists, to refuse any involvement of any kind in abortion. Now, one's employer can even deny abortion coverage.[35] Bush covers up his anti-woman policies – with a female front. All five cabinet women in his first term were known conservatives or neoliberals, especially Labor Secretary Elaine Chao, Secretary of the Interior Gale Ann Norton, and Agriculture Secretary Ann Veneman. Bush's cowgirls obscure the reality of his anti-democratic politics, and carve a pictorial of a militarist womanhood as both normal and necessary.

All of Bush's cowgirls have been openly hostile to women-friendly movements of all sorts including affirmative action, and activist government intervention to end women's discrimination. Laura Bush spoke of democracy at the 2004 Republican convention and how hard it is to create. When she needed to talk about women and women's lives being better under her husband's watch she chose to speak of Afghanistan and Iraq, where she misrepresented the gains made by women and silenced the realities of war. Meanwhile the women of both countries are suffering enormously given the chaos and war in their countries. Although there are new opportunities they remain limited to middle-class and urban women. In Afghanistan warlords are in control once again. Only 10 percent of registered voters were women from the cities. Most women fear going outside, whether to work or to vote.[36]

Although violence towards women and Islamic extremism continues to be daunting to Afghan and Iraqi women, they also are founding women's shelters in Baghdad and Kirkuk. They continue to struggle creatively even though life for women in Iraq is deeply troubled. For many, life feels like it is going backwards. Now most women cover themselves in scarves and cloaks, something they did not do under Saddam. Most who voted in Afghanistan wore the burqa, the blue body wrap that once was used to symbolize their oppression.[37] The daily violence does not move them towards democracy but back inside their homes. Strangely, the hijab protects them more than American-style democracy while they lose rights that were formerly their own.

Most starkly, President Bush's request for $87 billion for Iraq had no mention of funding for women's programs. He failed to endorse UN

Resoluton 1325 calling for women's inclusion in peacekeeping and reconstruction efforts. He refused to ratify CEDAW (the UN Convention for the Elimination of Discrimination Against Women), which is basically a global bill of rights for women guaranteeing their education and rights in the workplace. In all, 177 countries around the world have signed the CEDAW treaty. The US stands with Iran and Somalia against it.

Instead Bush has granted $10 million in loans to several groups, including the Independent Women's Forum (IWF) to sponsor an "Iraqi Women's Democratic Initiative". The IWF was started by Lynne Cheney and Midge Decter, who were also supporters of Clarence Thomas's nomination to the Supreme Court. The IWF has lobbied in the United States against the Violence Against Women Act, disputes the factual validity of the wage gap, has opposed efforts to strengthen the enforcement of the Equal Pay Act, and challenges the need for Title IX to protect opportunity in sports for girls and women.[38]

Indeed, things are not good for women back home. Bush's policies undermine gender rights for women. Shortly after Bush took office he closed and downsized numerous government offices focused on women's interests and rights in the realm of work. Especially troubling, he closed the key office of the Women's Bureau in the Labor Department. Because of this, it is hard to find data on wage-earning women and wage discrepancies because the tracking is no longer being done. This dismantling of the Women's Bureau was done at the same time that Bush's cowgirls were speaking on behalf of the Afghan war and Afghan women's rights. Females in his administration are his cover.

The legal basis for equal opportunity for women at work has been vaporized and the equal pay initiative has been ended. The Department of Labor under Bush has repealed the regulations allowing paid family leave for those needing to care for sick children or elderly parents, and has initiated cuts in childcare. This has undermined the government-funded pre-school Head Start program for low-income children and made cuts in federal programs supporting after-school activities. Bush closed the White House Women's Office which was established in 1995 charged with coordinating policy initiatives related to women's lives.

Also: Attorney General Ashcroft appointed two members to the National Advisory Commission on Violence Against Women who have called for its demise; the administration has de-funded a majority of battered women's programs; and it has failed to respond to initiatives which focus on the need for gun control as a part of dealing with domestic violence.

In spite of the problem of sexual harassment and rape in the military the administration has limited the role of the Defense Advisory Committee on Women. A Bush appointee, Catherine Aspy, says of women in the military that they are unmarried teenage mothers using it as a welfare home – a charge that is factually untrue.

In the realm of judicial appointments the administration has selected nominees who do not support equal protection under the law; who oppose protection in sexual harassment; who undermine sexual discrimination legislation; who wish to overturn *Roe* v. *Wade*; who reject core civil rights doctrine. Bush has become well known for appointing males and females who are hostile to a women's right to reproductive choice. David Hager was appointed to head the Federal Drug Association – and does not believe in birth control. He was forced to quietly resign after his former wife documented allegations of continual sexual and emotional abuse involving repeated nonconsensual painful anal sex by him.[39]

Bush degenders sex and sexual equality in his attempt to mollify anti-imperial feminist claims for democracy. His politics of chimera continues to travel across the globe. Bush says he removed the Taliban and Saddam Hussein and ignores the horrific realities of these war-torn countries. A few schools have reopened in Afghanistan, but it is too dangerous for most girls to attend. Saddam is gone but most women's lives remain filled with fear.

Bush cut off funds to the United Nations Population Fund in all 142 countries in which it operates because of its connection to China and its abortion policies. Meanwhile the plans for midwife training in Algeria, a center to fight AIDS in Haiti and a maternal mortality reduction program in India all collapsed. Bush has banned the use of US aid in family planning programs not committed to abstinence. Meanwhile 500,000 women die in childbirth each year. Another 100 million suffer malnutrition, and 60 percent of girls across the globe cannot attend school. The Bush administration policies punish the most vulnerable, and the language of compassionate conservatism covers over this unconscionable crude use of power and empire.

When I travel elsewhere – to Korea, India, Cuba, Pakistan, and Egypt – the women I meet in these countries are clear that the only way their lives will improve is if the lives lived in their country improve and for that to happen the imperial policies of the Bush administration must end. They ask why women and feminists in the US cannot do a better job in saying no to Bush's policies of war and greed. They say: after all, you are a democracy.

Just in case this is not perfectly clear by now: I like girlie men and women and wish the Democrats were more girlie. Girlie people take into account the specifically gendered and racialized experiences and radically pluralize their viewings with these insights. This brings me be back to where I started. Bush's war has militarized women's rights rhetoric for authorizing war. Females and women have been militarized and masculinized in this process. The horrors of Abu Ghraib bespeak the gender bending and confusion of this war. Women have become both decoys and actors as this administration continuously remobilizes for war. Hatred is written with and on female bodies. The same party that ran a convention trying to humiliate the Democratic party as pussy-whipped women is the same administration that knew of the torture and humiliation at Abu Ghraib, Guantanamo, and Afghanistan. Women in the US must stand with the women across the globe against our own humiliation and theirs.

Bush won the 2004 election despite the fact that the US is losing the war in Iraq, despite the fact that there were no weapons of mass destruction; despite the fact that over 360 tons of explosives were stolen under US watch; despite the fact that a group of eighteen US soldiers said that they would not comply with their orders because they did not have the proper tanks; despite the repeated kidnappings and beheadings. Despite all the facts, Bush won. And female bodies were used to cover up and manipulate these truths. There is little comfort in the fact that by 2005 the US public had begun to criticize Bush and his war, because the Democrats are too scared to become the girlie people they need to be.

Hillary Clinton ups the ante on decoy politics from within the Democratic party as she carefully disavows commitments to feminism. Both Condi and Hillary do the bidding of imperial democracy for their parties, while Renel Marc Gerecht, a former CIA Middle East specialist, says that in 1900 women didn't have the vote in the US either. And he says: "I mean, women's social rights are not critical to the evolution of democracy."[40] The problem is not simply Bush, or the Republicans, but neoliberal forms of gendered masculinity often in female face.

Gender decoys allow democracy to parade around in drag. Hillary didn't bake cookies, was disciplined and no-nonsense, while Bill was depicted as out of control: too much food, too much sex, too much talking, just like a woman. Laura Bush is the teacher: educated and focused and a non-drinker. She is the devoted wife but the brains in the couple. Bush rides around in a cowboy hat and males seem macho and silly. The resexing, but not the degendering of the privatized nation of global capital is in process.

Dislocating imperial feminism

It is really difficult to know in what ways Afghan and Iraqi women's lives have changed for the better, if at all, since the initial demise of the Taliban and the removal of Saddam Hussein. In both instances aspects of tyrannical regimes were removed, but neither regime was fully destroyed. More troubling is what has been reconstructed in their place. In Afghanistan the Taliban has gained a new hold with dire consequences for women's and girl's lives. Some of the initial changes were overstated to begin with, especially for women living in rural areas. Horrible crime and poverty still are the predominant realities alongside the presence of US forces. The lives of women are still highly militarized as they continue to live in a war zone, many as refugees.

In the 2003 Afghan constitution there was no mention of women's rights. Yet in the 1964 constitution women had a right to education, equal pay for equal work, and freedom to vote.[41] The newest Afghan constitution now disallows discrimination of any kind; yet "no law can be contrary to the beliefs and provisions of the sacred religion of Islam".[42] However, it is a political issue who decides the appropriate interpretation of Islam here. Ninety-nine percent of Afghan women are Muslim, and while many of them are devoutly religious they also believe that their rights as women are available to them in the Quran.

The Pershmerga Force for women, founded in 1996, are a Kurdish militia group who defended Iraqi Kurdistan, a northern sector of Iraq, as a self-rule enclave. These women, five hundred strong, supported the US invasion to oust Saddam and faced death to do so. In both Iraq and Afghanistan there have been rich histories of women's activism – yet females are more often than not presented as passive. Yet veiling, in whatever particular form, was not a traditional and established part of Afghan women's lives. The history of the chador, or hijab, or burqa is instead a history of the gendering of Islamic and/or Muslim women.

38 Ann Lewis, "Antifeminists for Iraqi Women", *Gadflyer*, October 14, 2004, available at *http://www.alternet.org/story/20189*.

39 Ayelish McGarvey, "Dr Hager's Family Values", *The Nation*, vol. 280, no. 21 (May 30, 2005), p.13.

40 As quoted in Maureen Dowd, "My Private Idaho", *New York Times*, August 23, 2005, p. A17.

41 Amy Zalman, "Women, Citizens, Muslims", *Women's Review of Books*, vol. xxi, no. 5 (February 2004), p. 21. Also see Sunita Mehta, ed., *Women for Afghan Women* (New York: Palgrave, 2002).

42 Carolyn Maloney, "A Better Future for Afghan Women?", *Ms*, vol. xiv, no. 1 (Spring 2004), p. 33.

43 Elisabeth Armstrong and Vijay Prashad, "Solidarity Across Movements", in Riley and Inayatalluh, eds., *Interrogating Imperialism*.

44 Hamida Ghafour, "Opening Afghan Eyes with Mascara and Beauty Classes", *Los Angeles Times*.com, April 4, 2004.

45 Babak Dehghanpisheh, Eve Conant and Rod Nordland, "Iraq's Hidden War", *Newsweek*, March 7, 2005, pp. 21–5.

46 "Their Last Letters Home", *Glamour*, December 2004, pp. 172–4.

47 Dyan Mazurana, "Women in Armed Opposition Groups Speak on War, Protection and Obligations under International Humanitarian and Human Rights Law", a report of a workshop organized in Geneva, August 26–29, 2004.

48 Available at: *http://www.wluml.org*.

49 Anissa Helie, "Occupied Territories/Occupied Bodies", unpublished paper, May 2005.

50 Nancy Hatch Dupree, "A Socio-Cultural Dimension: Afghan Women Refugees in Pakistan", in Ewan Anderson and Nancy Hatch Dupree, eds., *The Cultural Basis of Afghan Nationalism* (London: Pinter, 1990), pp. 128, 130; and her ' The Women of Afghanistan', in *Writers Union of Free Afghanistan*, vol. 5, no. 2 (April/June, 1990), pp. 30–41.

51 Saba Mahmood, *Politics of Piety* (New York: Princeton University Press, 2005), pp. 10, 15, 34.

52 Kari Browne, "Status Report: Egyptian Women 2003", *Ms,* vol. xiii, no. 3 (Fall 2003), p. 38.

53 "Israel and the Occupied Territories: Conflict, Occupation and Patriarchy, Amnesty International Report. Available at: *http://web.amnesty.org/library*.

54 Susan Muaddi Darraj, "Palestinian Women, Fighting Two Battles", *Monthly Review Press*, vol. 56, no. 1 (May, 2004), pp. 24, 25, 28.

55 Nazila Fathi, "Iran Moves to Roll Back Rights Won by Women", *New York Times*, September 19, 2004, p. A17.

56 Patricia McFadden, "Issues of Gender and Development from an African Feminist Perspective", Lecture at the Center for Gender and Development

Studies", University of the West Indies, Bridgetown, Barbados, November 2000. Available at: *www.wworld.org/programs/regions/africa*.

57 Bernedette Muthien, "Queerying Borders: An Afrikan Activist Perspective", available from *info@engender.org.za*. To be published in the *Journal of Lesbian Studies*, 2007.

58 *www.refusersolidarity.net*.

59 *http://nobelprize.org/peace/laureates/2004/index.html*.

60 Valentine Moghadam, *Globalizing Women; Transnational Feminist Networks* (Baltimore: Johns Hopkins, 2005), pp. 14, 52.

Index